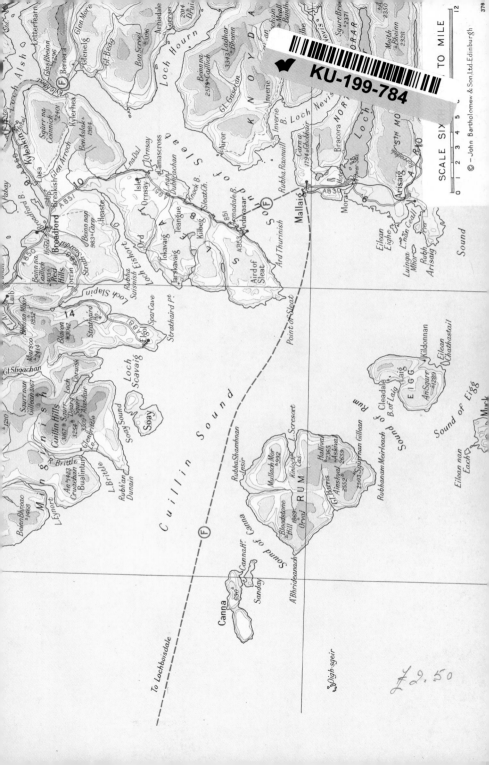

379

© – John Bartholomew & Son.Ltd.Edinburgh.

SCALE SIX   , TO MILE

0 1 2 3 4 5

12

£2.50

Scottish Mountaineering Club
District Guide Books

THE ISLAND OF SKYE

General Editor: MALCOLM SLESSER

SCOTTISH MOUNTAINEERING CLUB
DISTRICT GUIDE BOOKS

THE
Island of Skye

by Malcolm Slesser, PH.D., FRGS

THE SCOTTISH MOUNTAINEERING TRUST

EDINBURGH

First Published in Great Britain in 1970 by
THE SCOTTISH MOUNTAINEERING TRUST
369 High Street, Edinburgh 1, Scotland

Copyright © 1970 by The Scottish Mountaineering Trust

First Edition 1923
Reprinted 1931, 1935
Second Edition 1948
First Edition New Series 1970

Designed for the Scottish Mountaineering Trust by
West Col Productions

WHOLESALE DISTRIBUTORS
West Col Productions
1 Meadow Close
Goring on Thames
Reading Berks   RG8 OAP

SBN 901516 26 0

ERRATUM

Illustrations Nos. 8, 28, 36, 38, 42 and 50, credited to D. J.
Bennet, are in fact reproductions of the original photographs
in W. A. Poucher's *Magic of Skye*, and to whom they are now
acknowledged.

Set in Monotype Plantin Series 110 and Grotesque 215
and printed in Great Britain by Cox & Wyman Ltd,
London, Reading and Fakenham

CONTENTS

ILLUSTRATIONS

PLATES

DIAGRAMS AND FIGURES

ACKNOWLEDGEMENTS

This guide book was promoted by the guide book committee of the Scottish Mountaineering Club, who asked me, the editor for general guides, to write it. I am much indebted to Dr. Arthur Ewing, who willingly expanded his remit as editor of climbing guides, to examine and improve the manuscript.

In the course of writing the guide I became aware of the amount of preparatory work already embarked upon by others with a view ultimately to producing such a guide as this. I am sorry that when the decision was taken to produce this guide this information was not known so that these efforts could have been co-ordinated with my own, and the production made fuller and richer. I am most indebted to Myles Morrison who passed on material written on the Flora of Skye by Alf Slack, which is included intact.

Naturally in respect of the Black Cuillin I have leant heavily on the original SMC work by Messrs. Steeple, Barlow, MacRobert and J. H. B. Bell, and its up-dating by W. McKenzie. I am also most grateful for the timely production of the new SMT rock climbing guides to Skye written by J. Simpson and edited by Arthur Ewing. The perspective and information offered by these new guides has been most useful to me.

To the many people who responded to my requests for photographs I owe thanks. Those whose photographs were used are given due credit in the contents page.

I am grateful to the Isle of Skye Tourist Association for much information, and to Mr. D. McLean of Staffin for information on the weather of the islands. I am most grateful to Professor Derek Thomson for his opinion on the meaning and spelling of certain Gaelic words.

PREFACE

THIS GUIDE is written to assist all those who wish to know the mountains and hills of the Island of Skye. It is hoped it will serve both climbers and the walkers. The climber will, of course, seek detailed information in the SMT rock climbing guides, recently republished (1969) in entirely new form. The mountaineer accustomed to his own route finding will find ample information to enable him to penetrate into the best regions of the mountains and find worthy climbs. The walker will find cautionary information to guard him from over-extending his activities, and to enable him, as far as possible, to penetrate into the mountains, without indulging in rock-climbing.

There are a thousand eminences in Skye, and not all are described. The guide is restricted to those peaks which, in the author's opinion, are worthy of ascent. They vary in height from 207 ft. to the highest of the Cuillin. Armed with this guide even the most determined rock climber should be able to find something to pass away a rainy spell in the high Cuillin, and perhaps find a new interest in the drier north of the island, or in the subtle shapes and forms of the lesser hills.

The Scottish Mountaineering Trust (SMT) welcomes any new information that readers may care to send, and of course, a note of errors and omissions. Readers seeking up to date information on climbing in Skye should purchase the Scottish Mountaineering Club Journal (published annually about May) and available through bookstalls and mountain equipment dealers.

FOREWORD

THE FIRST EDITION of the Island of Skye Guide was issued in 1923 and a revised edition in 1948. During the next decade many new routes were made on the rock faces of the Black Cuillin and in 1958 a separate Climber's Guide was published, and with the continuing exploration of previously unclimbed routes, a third edition has just been issued.

The Guide Book Committee of the Scottish Mountaineering Club felt that there were many visitors to the Island who would welcome a Guide with more general information about the Cuillins and the many other hills of Skye.

It was felt this Guide should be on sale by early 1970. They were most fortunate in obtaining the services of Malcolm Slesser, who undertook to meet an early deadline.

The Committee hope that this Guide will enable the many visitors to the Island to plan their holiday to best advantage.

W. B. Speirs, *December* 1969

WARNING TO HILLWALKERS

The Guide Books issued by the Scottish Mountaineering Club describe routes which range from difficult climbs to what are, in fine summer weather, mere walks. All must judge for themselves whether they have the experience necessary for carrying out their intended expeditions within a reasonable time, remembering that conditions may quickly change a simple walk into a serious undertaking. Safe walking on the hills involves properly constituted and adequately equipped parties, reasonably prepared for unexpected difficulties, and having strength of mind to turn back when desirable. Experienced climbers, even when merely expecting to walk, wear boots suitably soled for rock climbing and carry reserves of food and clothing, 1-inch map, compass, torch, a rope (unless it is certain not to be required), and an ice axe when there is any chance of meeting snow or ice. Others cannot afford to take less.

Accidents in recent years call for this notice; for not only have local residents been called away from their ordinary vocations and caused trouble and anxiety, but experienced climbers have been summoned from long distances to form rescue parties. It will be understood that such assistance must not be regarded as always available, and that local workers may reasonably expect to be adequately paid.

Some common causes of difficulty are:

Failure to judge length of time required for expedition. Unduly slow or incompetent companion. Illness: sprained ankle. Unexpectedly difficult ground. Mist: darkness: snowstorm: loss of way. High wind (especially on ridges). Extreme cold: frostbite. Members of a party becoming separated.

Deep soft snow: steep hard snow. Except on the level, snow, whether hard or soft, necessitates an ice-axe for safety. Soft snow may freeze hard in a few hours and so involve step-cutting. Avalanches, walking over cornices.

Ice-glazed rocks or paths. One shower may cause this and the ice may be invisible.

Sudden spates, rendering burns uncrossable or only safely crossable with a rope.

MOUNTAIN RESCUE

In case of accident inform the Police at Portree. There are stretchers at Coruisk hut (locked) and Glen Brittle House.

FIRST AID AND RESCUE

There is a rescue post at Glen Brittle, with three stretchers and First Aid rucksacs.

At the Coruisk Memorial hut (Grid reference 487197) is a stretcher and First Aid kit, but this is not a full mountain rescue kit. Since the hut is locked, it is only available when the hut is in use.

There are public telephones at such key points as Sligachan hotel, Glen Brittle House, Elgol, Broadford and Torrin. When assistance of any sort, such as doctor or ambulance is needed, Dial "O" (procedure in 1969) and ask for the service. If the police and assisted mountain rescue service is required, phone the police at Portree (Portree 4 and 163).

Walkers and climbers should be aware that their unintentional absence from their camp or hotel may result in emergency services being brought into action unnecessarily. If you are benighted or late in returning be sure that you telephone the police to announce your safe return in case a search party is looking for you. It is always a wise policy to let someone know where you are heading, with some idea of your expected time of return.

In the Cuillins, the compass is generally unreliable, and may on occasion be 80 degrees out.

PROPRIETARY AND
SPORTING RIGHTS

The Scottish Mountaineering Trust desire to impress upon all those who avail themselves of the information given in their Guide Books that it is essential to consider and respect proprietary and sporting rights.

During the shooting season, from about the beginning of August to the middle of October, harm can be done in deer forests and on grouse moors by people tramping through them. During this period walkers and climbers should obtain the consent of the local stalkers and gamekeepers before walking over shooting lands. At times it is not easy to recognize what constitutes shooting lands. In cases of doubt it is always wise to ask some local resident.

It should also be noted that many of the roads in the upper glens were made and are maintained by the proprietors, who do not acknowledge a public right to motor over them, though they may follow the lines of established rights-of-way. It is, however, frequently possible to obtain permission to motor over some of them, but, as the situation is liable to change, local inquiries should be made in advance.

INTRODUCTION

IT IS said that no part of the Island of Skye is more than five miles from the sea. It sticks out of the west coast of northern Scotland like a lobster's claw ready to snap at the fish bone of Harris and Lewis. Once an end point of a journey, it is today the highway to the outer Hebrides, and the number of visitors has risen accordingly.

While the island is an obvious sixty miles long, its breadth, to quote Murray, 'is beyond the ingenuity of man to state'. No less than fifteen major sea lochs bite into the land. The sea pervades the island, leaving its salty tang on the wind that blows more frequently than not. It is visible from every hill top, a restless force that dominates every moment, bathing the land in constant warmth.

One cannot yet fly there, though an emergency strip exists at Broadford. One must go by sea. And if the magic of Skye grips you at all, the wand will have struck even before you leave the mainland, when with the sound of Sleat before you, the receding ranges of the most mountainous island in Scotland are suddenly visible. This is a moment of adventure whether you see rain-drenched hillsides revealed in all their black oiliness, or the Sound is heaving in white horses whipped into fury by an ebb tide, or it is one of those still days of early summer when the hills seem to throw off their age-old stiffness and shimmer as if gently awakening. No matter which, one's urge to cross the Sound is compulsive.

To the mountaineer and walker who has never been there, Skye spells only one word: the Black Cuillins. Of all mountains in the British Isles, these have the most dramatic form. They present acres of vertical rock to fascinate the climber, and a ridge whose persistent narrowness and ever-changing character is the ultimate challenge to the hill-walker. But to represent Skye as the Cuillins is unfair to the lesser hills around. Hills, which in another location would be tramped on eagerly, whose declivities would bring forth legend and song, and whose ramparts would engage the new leagues of climbers. Skye is the complete island, and if because of its monstrous topographical shape it is a long road to anywhere, one can equally go there a hundred times and still find something new.

Almost irrationally it has an east, west, south and northern aspect. Each presents a different world. Westwards lie the Uists, with Ronay no more than 14 miles from Neist Point; Lochmaddy is a mere 18 miles from Dunvegan head. A northern seascape is always different, and here Harris and Lewis dominate the skyline. To the east is the wall of the mainland hills astoundingly complex from this aspect, so that in the course of a day's hill-walking the scene never for one moment stays static. And southwards! Into the eye of the Sun stand the silhouettes of the inner isles and the sea stacks. On a calm day the texture of the sea reveals every current, every subterranean rock.

The climate of Skye is simple. To those accustomed to the weather in London, Geneva or Glasgow, Skye continually confounds. It is elemental. It can have a three-month drought. It can rain continuously for a week. The Skyeman, when asked by a tourist if it always rained, replied that it occasionally snowed. And, one might add, very occasionally at that. To catch the Cuillin in full winter regalia is luck indeed. But it rains little more than most other places, and a lot less than the western mainland. Out of the bitterest western gale and driven rain can emerge an evening of unparalleled beauty. Here the weather fronts hold their sharp demarcations. The bright spell is bright. Squally means your tent needs all the holding down you can provide. To climb in a westerly gale is like being pumped full of ozone. When the summer anti-cyclone settles on the island, the heat even at three thousand feet may be oppressive. Flies may dance ritually in the shade of mountain crests. Distance is no hindrance to noise. In such a day in May I have heard cuckoos calling simultaneously in Glen Brittle and Loch Scavaig.

Skye is no place for those who cannot take the rough with the smooth. Indeed after the first visit it is no place for those who do not accept its many virtues and ignore its defects. For sheer utter bleakness almost nowhere in the world can compare with Glen Drynoch in heavy rain. The capacity of Skye peatland to retain water after weeks of drought is worthy of special research. The island has few sandy beaches, and even her best are no competition to those of the mainland and other islands. Her midges outclass the worst of Amazon beasties. But all this the reader will have to judge for himself. If he once tastes the best of Skye he will never be satisfied until he has returned, and returned again.

Layout

In this introduction is given all the general information about the island. The various mountainous regions of the island are dealt with in turn under the districts in which they occur. Naturally the Black Cuillin of Minginish form the largest group and thus the bulk of this guide. Each district forms a chapter. Where, as in Minginish, the detail is too great for one chapter, each corrie is given a separate section. To find details of a district, look up the appropriate chapter. To find details of a particular mountain, look up the index. All climbs are not listed as they are dealt with in detail by the *Cuillin Rock Climbing Guide* (J. Simpson) published in two volumes by the Scottish Mountaineering Trust, but selected climbs are given in broad outline, and when shown on a diagram, bear the route number on the rock guide. Conventional British rock climbing gradings of Easy (E), Moderate (M), Difficult (D), Very Difficult (VD), Mild Severe (MS), Severe (S) and Very Severe (VS) have been adopted.

Maps

The island lies between Lat 57° 44′ N and 57° 03′ N. Its most westerly point is Long 6° 46′ W and its most easterly 5° 38′ W. Due to its shape it requires four OS one inch maps to convey its topography. These are: Seventh Series, sheets 24, 25, 33 and 34. The major part of the Black Cuillin are shown on Sheet 33. Published recently is the OS 2½-inch to the mile map in two sheets that cover the main part of the Black Cuillin, and is extremely useful to the climber. The Number is NG 42/52. The SMT have also produced a 3-inch to the mile map in two colours showing useful routes.

The territory is conveniently covered by Bartholemew's half-inch to the mile sheet 54, Skye and Wester Ross, but the lower portion of the Island (not including the Cuillin, for which region this map is on too small a scale) is shown in Sheet 50, Arisáig and Lochaber.

The Ordnance Survey six-inch to the mile map gives a remarkable degree of detail, indicating in many instances actual buttresses. The SMT are projecting a detailed colour large-scale map scheduled for publication in 1970.

Access

There are five sea routes to Skye from the Scottish mainland. Three of them serve cars. Up to date timetables should be consulted, and sources are listed below.

PASSENGERS:
Mallaig/Portree
Messrs. McBrayne Ltd., run a service four times a week during the summer direct to Portree with a stop at Kyle of Lochalsh and Raasay. The winter service has half this frequency.
Mallaig – Loch Coruisk – Mallaig. Daily Tourist boat in summer.

CAR FERRIES:
Mallaig/Armadale
McBrayne Ltd. Daily except Sundays. Approximately five services each way each day in summer, one in winter. Prices start at £1 6s. for an 11 ft. car and rise by length. Advance booking with cash accepted. Journey can be tied in with a through ticket permitting a visit to Mull via Oban, and onward to Loch Aline, through Skye and on to the outer Isles via Uig in Skye. Considerable reduction for return tickets. A bus from Broadford connects with these ferries. It is the shortest driving route from the South.

Glen Elg/Kylerhea
Independent operator. Functions only in summer and during daylight hours. Cheapest ferry to Skye, and scenically superb. Refreshment at mainland pier. Leave the A 87 at Shiel Bridge (bottom of Glen Shiel), and climb over the Mam Ratagan pass. A good steep road, with magnificent vistas. No Sunday service. Tel. Glenelg 224.

Kyle of Lochalsh/Kyleakin
British Railways. This service operates from approximately 07.00 to 23.15 and then periodically during night, using a shuttle service of up to three drive-on-ferries. Queues can be enormous in high summer, but shops and restaurants are at hand. Operates a limited service on Sundays (cancelled in 1969 but will probably re-commence).

TRAINS:
Trains from the south reach Mallaig via Fort William and Kyle of Lochalsh via Inverness.

BUS:

Glasgow/Fort William/Portree – Friday 22.00 north, Saturday 09.00 south. Wallace Arnold – Tel. 041-DOU-5662.

Edinburgh/Pitlochry/Portree – each Saturday. Eastern Scottish Omnibuses.

Principal Bus Services: For details consult timetables or phone Portree 47, unless otherwise indicated.

Armadale/Portree: There is a periodic bus service on week days taking two hours. It passes Broadford and Sligachan.

Kyleakin/Portree: There is a periodic bus service on week days taking 1½ hours. It passes Broadford and Sligachan.

Broadford/Elgol (for Loch Coruisk): One bus to Broadford in morning, return to Elgol in afternoon. Second service in summer.

Portree/Staffin and Kilmaluag: Daily at 17.30 and extra service on Tuesday, Thursday and Saturday

Portree/Uig: Daily 17.00 and extras in high season.

Sligachan/Carbost/Glen Brittle: Week days during school term, otherwise Friday only. Tel. Carbost 223.

Carbost/Fiskavaig: As above.

Sligachan/Dunvegan: Once daily, westward in afternoon, eastward in morning.

Dunvegan/Duirinish Peninsula: Three per week.

Soay: Boat every second Tuesday. Tel. Mallaig 33.

Raasay: Mallaig/Kyle/Portree steamer calls on in Tuesday, Thursday, Friday, Saturday. Boat may be hired from Peinchorron or Sconser. Tel. Raasay 226. Car hire available on Raasay. Tel. Raasay 206.

BOAT HIRE:

Glen Brittle: McDonald, P. O. Glen Brittle. Tel. Carbost 231.

Elgol: R. McKinnon, 2 Elgol; L. McIntosh, 1 Elgol; A. McLean, Glas na Kille, by Elgol.

Raasay: A. Nicolson. Tel. Raasay 226.

Kyle of Lochalsh: McLean & McRae, Kyle.

Mallaig: A. McLennan. Tel. Mallaig 14. B. Watt. Tel. Mallaig 33.

Dunvegan: Robertson, Dunvegan Hotel. N. D. Henderson, Glendale. Tel. 258

Uig: Enquire Uig Hotel or Post Office.

CAR HIRE (Telephone numbers only):
Portree: N. Beaton, Portree 2. E. Morrison, Portree 96.

Dunvegan: P. Carson, Dunvegan 273.

Glen Brittle: W. Sutherland, Carbost 223.

Broadford: Sutherland's Garage, Broadford 210.

Kyleakin: A. McLean, Kyleakin 210.

Isle Ornsay: D. McKinnon, Isle Ornsay 227.

This list is not exhaustive.

TIMETABLES:
The most comprehensive information is that issued by the Highlands & Islands Development Board, 6 Castle Wynd, Inverness. Tel. 0463-34171. The Board issues the booklet: 'Getting Around in the Highlands and Islands – 4. Skye and Approaches'. 6d.
It is obtainable from the Board or the Skye Tourist Association, Portree. Add postage. It is on sale throughout the Highlands and Islands.

ACCOMMODATION:
Hotel and Boarding Houses
The Skye Tourist Association, Portree, produce a list stating prices and details. No grading.
Bed and Breakfast
These are numerous.
Campsites with facilities:
By the beach, Glen Brittle.
Breakish campsite, between Kyleakin and Broadford.
Blairmore, Broadford.
Marrapool, Broadford.
Ullinish Lodge, Struan.
Torvaig, by Portree.

Caravanning:

Caravans are a serious obstruction on Skye roads, and those who do take them should be at some pains to assist other traffic to pass them.

Camping

There are a few organized camping sites on the island, notably at Portree, Broadford, Dunvegan and Glen Brittle. Though the island is thinly populated and has an enormous coastline, it is not always easy to find camping-at-large that is attractive. There is a good deal of croft land that is suitable, and application to the crofter would in all probability result in permission. Frequently superb camping can be had by those willing to carry a camp a few hundred yards. Camping sites of worth by the road are few. It is best to look for old roads, such as the old road from Loch Ainort-head to Sconser, or to dead end roads, of which there are a great many. The presence of unfenced greensward doesn't imply a public right to use it, and the profusion of notices asking people not to spread litter or dump rubbish is a measure of the rising antagonism to the litter-lout. In most people's minds the camper is thought to be the culprit, though in fact it is the picnicker.

Skye and the visitor

The Sgitheanach, the people of Skye, are of Celtic origin. Their language is Gaelic, and it enshrines a culture older than English. For the older generation it is still the normal vehicle for communication. For the most part the younger people are bi-lingual, and English is the language of commerce. To the Skyeman, as to the man from the Outer Isles, a Sassunach is anyone south of the Highland Line, and is not really a name for an Englishman.

To appreciate the Skyeman's attitude to the visitor one must remember that the tourist invasion has not yet worked through one generation, and that old customs and standards remain. There is as yet no 'fun industry', and palpable inefficiencies and inadequacies abound. They abound partly because this is the way of life forced on the Skye people, and the bustling visitor looking for the raucous entrepreneurs of the world's more developed tourist areas will come away disappointed. The people of Skye live in a harsh climate, they are toughened by it, and the tourists' need of central heating and private bathrooms seems absurd to a people whose rooms may be heated by peat dug from their own moors, or who have still to enjoy the luxury of good radio reception in their own tongue.

All this does not imply that the Skyeman is backward or even unwilling to take advantage of the tourist invasion. But the islander lacks some confidence, and it is little wonder. Generations of U.K. governments have treated the Island people contemptuously, and though the various Crofting Acts have brought a certain security of tenure to the crofter and his family, and the Department of Agriculture for Scotland has become his best friend, the organization of an economy from and based on London has steadily destroyed a way of life and put nothing in its place. It is no longer possible to live off a croft, whose income is likely to bring in £100 per annum. In two world wars Skye gave all too generously of its young men, and a measure of its contribution is that 84 major-generals have come out of the Skye population. The only significantly practical contribution in 260 years to keeping young Skye people working and developing the islands for themselves has been through the recently formed Highlands and Islands Development Board.

The visitor will often find that arts and crafts, a fancy shop for souvenirs or a delicatessen is being run by incomers. The suggestion or even the implication may be that the Skye people lack the driving force to help themselves or step onto the band wagon. A boat advertized for Elgol may not run, and irritated tourists may have to go home with a wasted journey. Some thrusting driving Yorkshireman would have done it better and kept his schedules. But be tolerant, visitor. The hospitality, the kindness and the tolerance of the Skye people has been abused time and time again in the past. The birth of a new confidence takes time. We see signs of it now, but at the same time other things are going to rot. All over the island crofts are being reduced to the level of houses. The land is reverting to bog. To look across a moor to some well kept croft, its newly cut hay field gleaming lime green amongst the rank vegetation around, is to sight an oasis. The old get no younger, and this is an old, very old island.

Weather

A weather forecast for the whole of Skye is as likely to be correct as one for the whole of Europe. The differences between the north and south, or the east and the west of the island are significant. The climber sitting out the unrelenting rain and low level mist in Glen Brittle may find Staffin in bright sun. But then he may not. The island weather is complicated by the extent of the fluctuation from average. For example, May, which over many years averages out as the driest month, saw 3 inches of rain fall in 24 hours in 1958. The following account of the weather is due to the records kept by Mr. D. McLean, Headmaster at Staffin, and very kindly made available to the SMT.

RAINFALL

The first and most important aspect of the weather is to distinguish the north from the south of the island. Broadford, in the lee of the big hills, has a rainfall about twice that of Staffin in the north (see table 1), whose climate is closer to that of the Outer Hebrides. This is true of wet and dry years. Table 2 gives data taken over twenty years at Staffin. One can see at once the wide swings from the average, but an order of wetness does emerge. The months in increasing order of (average) wetness are:—

(Driest) May, April, March, February . . . September January/ November, October, December (wettest).

There are no figures from Glen Brittle, but a roughly similar order of months would be expected there, though the rainfall in the high Cuillin and Coruisk can be expected to considerably exceed even that of Broadford.

Table 2 shows that the highest figures are for Broadford in September: 12·1 inches. Yet these are not tremendous figures by west Highland standards. In December 1966 Achnashealach had 21·15 inches, and Kinlochewe 22·33 inches. Table 2 shows that in nine cases the heaviest downpour within 24 hours exceeds the normal monthly average. Looking at the driest months (for Staffin) the record shows that six years in twenty had less than 0·7 inches rain.

What it all boils down to is this:—

1. The north tends to be drier than the south.
2. The weather can be appalling or wonderful at literally any time of the year. The odds are on your side in May, and against you in December.

WIND

The wind force over the island tends to be much the same in exposed places. Mr. McLean made a study of the winds over five years from 1964 to 1969, recording the incidence of winds of force 6 (25 m.p.h.) or over, and their direction. The south wind is commonest, the west the next commonest, and the S.W. the third commonest. And they frequently bring winds of force 6 and above. Next most likely is the N.W. wind, with a very low incidence of high wind from the north-east or south-east. There are traditionally high winds in March when the incidence at force 6 is twice the average. Wind is the island's chief bug-bear. Winds of 80 m.p.h. have been recorded on the island, but these do not match record high winds elsewhere, and one might summarize the situation by stating that the island is windy, with still or light air a rarity rather than the normal, but excessive wind is extremely rare.

SUNSHINE

Sunshine is psychologically the most important element in the weather to the out-of-doors man. Table 3 gives a 20-year sunshine record expressed in terms of 'bright days' and not in cumulative hours. Skye is far enough north to have almost continuous daylight or twilight throughout the 24 hours at mid-summer. The total hours of sunshine possible at this time of year to a site exposed to east and west is thus considerable. The table shows that April was (in 1949) the dullest month, while in 1966 it was almost the brightest. It is clear that winter is just as likely to be bright as summer, and anyone who has enjoyed a spell of clear winter weather in Skye can testify what an exquisite experience it is. In such weather a record low humidity of 27% has been recorded (70 to 85% is normal).

Even 'bad' years have their bright spots. The summer of 1966 was one of the poorest in recollection, yet April showed 184 hours sun, a five-year record. 1500 hours sunshine a year is considered a high figure in Scotland, and is the average recorded by islands like Coll, and some east coast resorts. Yet Skye touched this figure in 1968. And in 1969 had passsed half that figure within the first half of the year.

Long sunshine spells are not common, but they do occur, there having been fifteen days in a row in June 1963, and almost as many in June 1967.

All in all, sun seems related to the length of the day with a tendency for a higher percentage of January to April days being sunny than summer days

TEMPERATURE

It is perfectly possible to have a January temperature in Skye greatly exceeding a mid-summer one. In January 1967 the warmest day was 50° F. June, July, August and September all showed minima of 40° F. 80° F. has been recorded in July, and 80° F. of frost is well below average minima for the coldest month. Table 4 shows twenty-years averages for Staffin

August emerges as marginally the hottest month, an attraction more than offset by the prevalence of midges. January is the coldest with December and February following closely. The long cold spells (temperature below freezing point) sought by the winter climbers are all too rare, but when they do come they can be outstanding. From January 23 to March 15, 1947, there were 52 days with continuous frost. December, January, February and March cold spells of a week to 10 days also occur from time to time. Unlike the mainland, April has never shown a cold spell. Hot spells, counted as days in which the noon-day temperature rose above 60° F. are less common than cold spells, and have occurred in various years from May to September.

The frustrating thing about Skye weather is the rapid change in temperature in winter. To find winter climbing one must almost live on the spot, or keep trying in the hope of eventual luck.

SNOW

Snow seldom lies. Indeed, years will pass by without snow lying at sea level in Skye. In the higher hills it accumulates through wind collection and packing, and will often out-last thaw periods. When snow does come to sea level in Skye, the effect is rather wonderful. The extended coastline, which is everywhere visible, imparts wonderful horizontal patterns to the view.

CONCLUSIONS

Skye weather is too fickle to make hard and fast plans. The very vagaries of the weather introduce an element of surprise, and often of delight. A lightning visit is the greatest risk, for it could rain the whole time. Over an extended period, say of ten days or more, provided one is prepared to move away from the high hills, one is likely to have a fair quota of fine sunny days. The greatest chance of dry weather is in May. In rock climbing, when it is often not so much the weather of the moment, as the weather of the past fortnight that dictates the condition of the climb, clearly the end of the dry winter period of late May and early June offers the best chances on east or north facing rocks. Coireachan Ruadha takes days to come into condition; Coire Lagan a matter of hours.

The boggy terrain is, of course, thoroughly unpleasant in spells of heavy rain. The moisture retention means that a week or more of dryness is needed before the character greatly alters. Again late winter and early spring is the best time of all when dryness and frost may provide a firm delightful terrain. But even in the wettest weather spells, there are plenty Skye hills whose top soil is firm and well drained.

TABLE I

RAINFALL IN 1967 – SOME SKYE FIGURES

Month	Duntulm	Staffin	Portree	Broadford	Carbost	For Comparison Stornoway
Jan.	4·50 in	3·43 in	5·97 in	4·93 in	9·26 in	3·64 in
Feb.	4·86	5·31	6·81	9·00	7·72	4·23
Mar.	8·39	11·88	14·76	19·60	14·11	7·95
Apl.	—	3·31	3·39	5·45	—	2·70
May	2·22	2·10	3·01	3·49	—	2·29
June	4·15	4·58	4·47	7·17	5·06	3·24
July	4·26	5·05	6·20	11·76	8·76	2·50
Aug.	3·58	2·71	3·71	4·67	—	2·46
Sept.	6·25	5·22	6·18	7·18	9·22	4·46
Oct.	10·06	11·64	15·87	16·50	—	8·67
Nov.	5·48	7·80	9·67	12·67	—	4·72
Dec.	5·81	6·68	9·10	10·93	11·10	5·03
Total	Approx. 65·21	69·71	89·14	113·35	—	51·89
5 Year Average	—	56·8 in	69·5 in	87·5 in	—	—

TABLE 2

RAINFALL – MONTHLY AVERAGES, ETC., STAFFIN SCHOOLHOUSE, ISLE OF SKYE

Month	(a) Average Rain Staffin "North End"	(b) Wettest Month	(c) Driest Month	(d) Heaviest Fall (24 hours).	(e) Average Rain (Approx.) Portree	(f) Approx. Average Rain Broadford	Driest Months
Jan.	5·25 in	11·41 in (1962)	1·33 in (1963)	1·63 in (1962)	8·1 in	9·2 in	(a) May
Feb.	3·41	6·70 (1961)	0·15 (1961)	1·65 (1956)	5·6	6·9	(b) April
Mar.	3·39	6·65 (1957)	0·68 (1964)	1·57 (1955)	4·6	6·0	(c) March
Apl.	3·30	6·28 (1965)	1·48 (1946)	1·17 (1947)	4·5	5·5	(d) Feb.
May	3·05	7·17 (1958)	0·36 (1951)	3·00 (1958)	3·7	4·1	
June	3·38	6·93 (1962)	1·09 (1949)	1·92 (1962)	4·0	5·2	*Wettest Months*
July	3·76	6·01 (1956)	1·42 (1955)	1·78 (1956)	4·7	5·7	(1) Dec.
Aug.	4·13	7·76 (1962)	0·12 (1947)	1·77 (1957)	5·4	7·1	(2) Oct.
Sept.	5·46	11·04 (1950)	3·08 (1959)	2·12 (1955)	6·7	12·1	(3) Nov.
Oct.	6·08	10·15 (1953)	0·45 (1946)	1·47 (1955)	8·5	11·7	(4) Sept. & Jan.
Nov.	5·81	12·82 (1953)	0·47 (1945)	1·88 (1956)	7·9	8·6	
Dec.	6·41	9·70 (1966)	2·85 (1947)	1·54 (1966)	7·5	9·1	

20 Years Aver. annual 56·5 in

Rain Total Year 1966 57·51 in

TABLE 3

SUNSHINE – STAFFIN, SKYE

Month	Average 'Bright' Days (Not by Hours) 20 Years		Aver. Hours Last 5 Years	Brightest (Hours)	Dullest Months 20 Years 1963/69 (to date)	
	Average 'Bright' Days	Brightest Days			Dullest Days	Dullest (Hours) Last 5 Years only
Jan.	9·4	15½/1963	—	—	4/1967	24 (1967)
Feb.	11·2	18½/1968	81	1968 (122)	4½/1965	38 (1965)
Mar.	13·2	18½/1956	103	1969 (147)	6/1945	70 (1966)
Apl.	14·5	18½/1966	160	1966 (184)	8/1949	123 (1964) 124 (1965)
May	15·8	20½/1967	171	1967 (207) 28 May – 13 June 1963 15 bright days (195 hrs. sun)	7/1956	129 (1965)
June	12·9	22/1968	177	1968 (243) June 1967 (10th/23rd) 14 bright days (152 hrs. sun)	4½/1952	118 (1965)
July	12·0	19/1949	138	1968 (185)	8/1967	88 (1967)
Aug.	14·4	20½/1968	175	1968 (265)	8/1951	85 (1963)
Sept.	9·9	12/1968	80	1968 (112)	4/1950	52 (1966)
Oct.	9·8	14½/1946	68	1965 (84)	4½/1949	48 (1968)
Nov.	8·5	15½/1952	51	1965 (83)	2½/1967	23 (1967)
Dec.	7·2	12/1961	—	—	2½/1952	23 (1968)

TABLE 4

TEMPERATURE °F – STAFFIN, ISLE OF SKYE

Month	(Average Covering) Noon shade	Warmest Month	20 Years Coldest Month	Noon Shade Warmest Day	Coldest Day
Jan.	40·2°F	45·1° (1950)	35·7° (1963)	52° (1950)	24° (1955)
Feb.	41·0	46·2° (1961)	33·5° (1947)	52° (1961)	26·5° (1969)
Mar.	44·9	48·0° (1961)	38·4° (1947)	59° (1948)	31° (1951)
Apl.	48·3	54·6° (1952)	45·3° (1950)	61·5° (1953)	32° (1968)
May	52·8	58·7° (1952)	49·9° (1949)	73° (1954)	39° (1967)
June	57·0	61·6° (1961)	54·8° (1964)	80° (1953)	45·5° (1964)
July	60·0	64·9° (1955)	55·4° (1962)	76° (1955)	50° (1948)
Aug.	60·2	67·5° (1955)	56·3° (1962)	76·5° (1955)	50·0° (1957)
Sept.	55·2	58·3° (1953)	52·1° (1952)	68·0° (1956)	44·0° (1954) (1964)
Oct.	50·7	53·9° (1951)	48·1° (1956)	64° (1958)	36° (1948)
Nov.	45·0	49·3° (1945)	41·4° (1965)	56° (1968)	31° (1952)
Dec.	41·5	45·4° (1953)	35·7° (1961)	54·5° (1948)	22° (1961)

C

Geology

G. S. JOHNSTONE, B.Sc., *Institute of Geological Sciences, Edinburgh*

Some 50–60 million years ago the land surface over what is now the Hebrides was an area of low relief made up from rocks representing most of the major groups now found in the Scottish Highlands. These comprised the ancient basement of Lewisian Gneiss whose rocks range up to 2600 million years and more in age, the Torridonian Sandstone deposited on that basement 900–700 million years ago and schists of the Moine Assemblage, probably representing Torridonian strata deformed, squeezed and recrystallized during the great Caledonian earth movements about 200 million years later. Rocks younger than the Torridonian consisted of Cambrian to Ordovician limestones and quartzites laid down about 600–450 million years ago with still younger Jurassic limestones sandstones and shales which are only about 150 million years old.

This, then, was the diverse constitution of the land which is now Skye at the beginning of the Tertiary Period, an epoch known in Central Europe for its great earth-movements which raised the Alps, but which in the north-western fringes of the continent and in the adjacent north Atlantic area was marked rather by intense volcanic activity. Evidence for this can be found not only in the Hebrides, but in Greenland, Jan Meyen, Spitzbergen and, of course, in Iceland, where volcanicity has persisted to this day.

In Skye the Tertiary volcanic activity first consisted of vast out-pourings of basaltic lavas, possibly in places associated with localized volcanoes, but in the main from several elongate fissures which tapped molten rock (magma) reservoirs deep in the earth's crust. A thickness of over 2500 ft. and probably much more of these lavas accumulated in Skye in a great number of relatively thin superimposed flows (in Mull a thickness of 6000 ft. is still preserved) and a volcanic plateau covered the whole island, possibly coalescing with similar accumulations over the adjacent Hebridean islands and mainland. Later on the activity appears to have become more localized on central volcanoes. In the Hebridean area remnants of these can be seen in Ardnamurchan, Rhum and, probably, in the great 'plutonic complex' of the Cuillins and Red Hills of Skye.

Little direct evidence for the Cuillin volcano now remains, but what is seen in the plutonic complex is rock formed from the soldification of the molten material which underlay it and which, at a late stage in the volcanic history of the area, rose up to invade the overlying lava pile. Although this magma was closely similar to that which poured out on the surface as basalt lavas it solidified in a different way. On the surface the lavas were quickly cooled and crystallized with fine grain to give a smooth-weathering black basalt; the same magma crystallizing in the depths of the plutonic complex cooled slowly, with resultant coarser grain, to give the beautifully rough-weathering, mottled gabbro which is so attractive to the climber.

The intrusion of the Cuillin pluton was probably accompanied, elsewhere in Skye, by the injection of large horizontal sheets (sills) of basalt and dolerite which are mainly found cutting the sedimentary strata underlying the lava pile. Within the Cuillins the gabbro mass is cut by innumerable thick and thin, more or less gently-inclined sheets and vertical 'dykes' of basalt and dolerite, the dykes extending well beyond the limits of the plutonic centre to traverse the whole of the island and well beyond. As commonly happens in such complexes as the Cuillins, the emplacement of the basic rock was followed by the uprise of a large mass of acid magma which broke through the Cuillin pluton to solidify as the granite mass of the Red Hills.

Following the close of the Tertiary igneous episode the Hebridean rocks were subjected to a period of erosion which has continued to the present day. The lava plateaux have been partially stripped to lay bare the underlying old land surface and the plutonic roots of the old volcanoes. The present distribution of the strata in Skye is shown on the accompanying sketch map.

Northern Skye. North of the Portree-Carbost-Glen Brittle road Skye is mainly made up of basalt lavas. Inland, these make up monotonous hills, commonly terraced (and sometimes flat-topped, as at McLeod's Tables) as a result of the more or less horizontal stratification of the lava flows. The scenery improves towards the seaboard, however, and fine sea-cliff features are found from place to place, notably at Dunvegan Head. Along the east side of Trotternish the cliff scenery, inland from the shore, is magnificent. Immense landslips have taken place in this area as the edges of the lava pile slid downwards and outwards on weak bands in the sedimentary strata lying below them, leaving lava precipices towering above the collapsed rubble as at the Storr, or forming stepped, fissured, blocks and pinnacles, as at the Quirang. In these cliffs the individual lava flows can be well seen. Unfortunately the rock is too broken and friable to provide good climbing. At Sheader about $1\frac{1}{2}$ miles east of

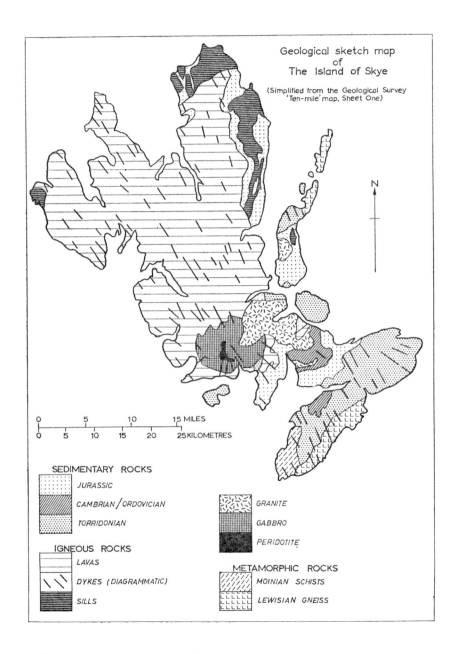

Geological sketch map
of
The Island of Skye

(Simplified from the Geological Survey
'Ten-mile' map, Sheet One)

N

0   5   10   15 MILES
0   5   10   15   20   25 KILOMETRES

SEDIMENTARY ROCKS

JURASSIC

CAMBRIAN / ORDOVICIAN

TORRIDONIAN

IGNEOUS ROCKS

LAVAS

DYKES (DIAGRAMMATIC)

SILLS

GRANITE

GABBRO

PERIDOTITE

METAMORPHIC ROCKS

MOINIAN SCHISTS

LEWISIAN GNEISS

Uig, another landslip, this time on a smaller scale, has resulted in a profusion of 'fairy hills' and is well worth a visit if one is passing time waiting for the Outer Isles ferry.

The sedimentary rocks and intrusive 'sills' underlying the lavas form the actual sea-cliffs east of the Portree-Staffin road. The sediments are rather inaccessible here but the 'Kilt Rock', which forms such a popular attraction south of Staffin, is a feature worth viewing. It is part of one of the large instrusive sills and in it the 'pleats' are made up of vertical basaltic columns which have resulted from contraction-fractures as the molten rock cooled – a phenomenon identical to that found on Staffa and at the Giant's Causeway of Antrim. On the west side of the Trotternish peninsula the sedimentary Jurassic strata become easily accessible in the bay south of Duntulm Castle, where certain bands within them can be seen to be packed with fossil shells. Many of these shells resemble modern 'oysters' and from this and other geological evidence it has been inferred that the rocks were laid down in an ancient estuary.

South-eastern Skye. South of the Broadford-Elgol road the country is made up mainly of the older Cambrian/Ordovician and Torridonian sedimentary rocks, together with the metamorphic Moine and Lewisian strata. The Torridonian and Moinian areas make up some pleasant, craggy, walking country. The Torridonian rocks, for the most part, represent deposits laid down by rivers, in lakes, and, possibly, in shallow sea areas adjacent to a former shore line.

On the west shore of Loch Slapin and near Elgol the younger group of sediments (Jurassic) is again well represented. These are largely sandstones and shales laid down in a sea close to an ancient shore line. The 'honeycomb' weathering of the sandstones around Elgol produces some odd (and photogenic) shapes in which to frame views of the Cuillin. This peculiar weathering is largely due to the leaching out of limey material in the rock. Spar Cave, at Glasnakille, is well worth a visit. There, a basalt dyke has cut the limey sandstone and, proving less resistant to wave action on the cliff face, has been eroded out to form a long, narrow fissure backed by a sizeable cave. Calcium carbonate ('spar') has been deposited over collapsed rubble in the cave floor to form attractive stalagmite formations. The cave is cut off except at low tide, so ask local advice about access. Visitors are asked not to damage in any way the stalagmite formations on the floor and the drip-pools. They take a long, long time to form! The adjacent sea cliffs hold promise for short, steep climbs on somewhat brittle rock, which requires delicate handling in places.

Central Skye. It is, of course, the plutonic mass of central Skye, and especially the Cuillin area, which will be of most interest to the readers of this account. While the general geological history and structure of the area are well known from the work of the late Alfred Harker, much detail still remains to be elucidated concerning the distribution and origin of the various varieties of 'gabbro' which makes up this great intrusive complex. From the climber's point of view, however, the only noticeable variant of gabbro is the reddish-brown peridotite which runs in an arc from the Garbh Choire, across Sgurr Dubh na Da Bheinn and down the west side of Sgurr Coire an Lochan. An outlying mass of this rock is also found on Bealach Buttress of the Corieachan Ruadha. Over much of its outcrop the peridotite is fantastically rough, both in its crystalline texture and in the detail of its almost sponge-like weathering, particularly well seen at Bealach a' Garbh Choire.

Although over the remainder of the Cuillin mass gabbro is the essential 'country' rock, the climber will find that on many of his routes he is encountering not the rough sound slabs of that material, but the smoother-textured basalt and dolerite of the later suite of intrusive vertical dykes and gently inclined sheets. Although these rocks are very hard, they tend to be more 'brittle' than gabbro. The dykes, especially, are strongly-jointed and yield more readily to weathering than does the tougher gabbro, tending to form gullies and chimneys. The inclined dolerite sheets vary in resistance to weathering, sometimes standing proud of the faces and at other times breaking out to form depressions. On the Coruisk side of the ridge these sheets form inclined slabs tilted towards the hollow of the valley. In general, the basalt and dolerite of these minor intrusions tend to be inferior to gabbro as a climbing rock. Unlike the latter they are slippery to rubber soles when wet and because of their brittle joint-fracturing have to be carefully examined when belaying or pegging. While the gabbro is normally very sound, in rare instances it can be found to be rotted, providing a crumbly, friable surface which has to be treated with caution, but this condition is normally very obvious.

The most continuous areas of gabbro are on Sron na Ciche, the Ghrunnda face of Sgumain and the slabs of the Dubhs. In these areas the rock is mainly of excellent quality. From Mhadaidh to Sgurr nan

Gillean the gabbro alternates with numerous inclined sheets of dolerite, while the Coire Lagan faces of Sgumain and Alasdair, whose inferior quality of rock compared with that of Sron na Ciche is proverbial amongst Skye rock-climbers, are largely of basaltic material. It is this same rock which makes the Thearlaich ridge of Mhic Coinnich so slippery to rubber soles in wet weather. The Inaccessible Pinnacle is partly gabbro sandwiched between two dykes, and much of the actual ascent on the long side is thus made on dyke material. It 'sits' on an inclined dolerite sheet, from which the surrounding gabbro, except for that included in the Pinnacle itself, has been stripped off.

It is this rapid variation in rock-type which gives rise to the serrated outline of the Cuillin, as almost all of the major depressions in the ridge (at least from Sgurr nan Gillian to Alasdair) and most gullies and chimneys are determined by dykes which have been more easily eroded than the gabbro they traverse. On the crest of the ridge itself the inclined sheets have in places proved more, and in places less, resistant than the gabbro they cut.

On the other hand the granite of the Red Hills, whose colour-contrast with the dark Cuillin gabbro is most striking when seen across the Coruisk and Sligachan valleys from the main ridge, is much less dissected by later intrusions. The granite weathers in a very uniform manner and this produces the typical smooth outlines characteristic of the group. The even disintegration of the rock leaves few steep faces.

Skye was at one time more or less completely covered by glaciers during the Pleistocene Ice Age, which commenced about two million years and terminated about ten thousand years ago. Features associated with this glaciation can be seen over all the island. Without doubt, however, they are best displayed in the bare corries of the Cuillin, which are probably products of the later, relatively recent stages of the Ice Age. These great depressions were gouged out by the accumulation within them of corrie glaciers whose former presence can be inferred from smoothed-off and pebble-scratched slabs around their sides and floors. Coire an Lochan, Coire Lagan, and Coire a' Ghrunnda all contain lochans which owe their presence to the over-erosion of the corrie floor at the expense of the corrie lip, a feature typical of cirques in present-day glaciated areas. The process of corrie formation, probably instituted in existing valleys, steepened the valley sides and headwalls to provide the cliffs for the mountaineer and, as they encroached from either side of the valley divide, they gradually narrowed the ridges, permitting an acceleration of the weathering of the rocky summits above the ice to produce the beautiful arêtes which are one of the delights of the hillwalker in the Cuillin.

BIBLIOGRAPHY

1904 Harker, A., 'The Tertiary Igneous Rocks of Skye'. A memoir of the Geological Survey, H.M.S.O.

1910 Peach, B. N. and Others, 'The Geology of Glenelg, Lochalsh and the South-East part of Skye'. A memoir of the Geological Survey. H.M.S.O.
(Both the above memoirs are out of print.)

1961 Richey, J. E., British Regional Geology, 'Scotland: the Tertiary Volcanic Districts'. A Handbook of the Geological Survey. H.M.S.O. (This is a cheap, relatively simple account of the major volcanic centres of the west Highlands – Rhum, Skye, Ardnamurchan, Arran – and is for those with a little geological knowledge.)

1966 Anderson, F. W., and Dunham, K. C., 'The Geology of Northern Skye'. A memoir of the Geological Survey. H.M.S.O.

Geological Maps on the scale of one-inch-to-one-mile. These are available through Ordnance Survey agents. Skye is covered by: Northern Skye (a special 'District' map comprising sheet 80 and parts of sheets 81, 90 and 91); Minginish (Sheet 70) and Glenelg (Sheet 71 – in press 1969).

Nomenclature

The spelling of the word 'Cuillin' has exercised the ingenuity of many generations. In 1549 it appears as Cuilluelum (Donald Munro), in 1560–1630 as Culluelun or Gulluin Hills, in 1703 as Quillin (Martin), in 1800 as Cullin (Robt. Jameson). Sir Walter Scott has it in 1814 as Quillen, and J. D. Forbes in 1836 gives it as Cuchullin Hills. The Ordnance Survey maps of the present day adopt Cuillin Hills. Although the Ordnance spelling has been followed in this book, the word 'Hills' has been omitted, in deference to the wish of the late Sheriff Nicolson.

Colin B. Phillip writes:

'There is considerable difference of opinion about the name Cuillin (as spelt in the Ordnance Survey). It used always to be Cuchullin in the old maps and books, and this is the form adopted by

Sir Walter Scott, no mean authority, with a leaning, however, to the traditional rather than the descriptive. Sheriff Nicolson called it A' Chuilionn, and certainly no greater authority on matters relating to Skye ever existed. The Irish antiquaries adhere to Sir Walter's version. I had a long argument once at Leenane on the subject with one of the best-known men, and he insisted that it *was* named after Cuchullin, Prince of Antrim, who learned the arts of war at Dansky Castle. I will not repeat the outline of the saga, as I might get it wrong. Personally, I think it is more likely that the Sheriff was right, as the Highlanders nearly always name places from their appearance or local peculiarity, and not after historical events or legends. Of course, there are exceptions to every rule. A' Chuilionn would point to the meaning being connected with hollies, whether after the (at present time) insignificant number of hollies on the Brittle slope near Coire a' Ghrunnda, or after the distant appearance of the range being "prickly" like holly leaves, it is hard to say. Is it not possible that the name is very old and not modern Gaelic at all? Once at the Devil's Bridge, in Wales, I met Dr. Hughes, D.D., of Carnarvon, who, in talking of the Welsh and Scottish place-names, was much struck on hearing the name Cuillin, saying, 'We have an old Celtic word, Coolin (spelling not vouched for), meaning worthless.' This, from a purely utilitarian point of view – the view most likely to be taken by the primitive inhabitants at their foot – the magnificent Cuillin certainly are, reminding me of an answer I once had in my pre-Glencoe days, when I asked an old keeper in Rannoch what Glencoe was like, "Oh! a nasty rough hole, wi' no feedin' in it at all", which, by the way, is a libel. I may mention that some of the inhabitants of Glen Brittle call the hills in Rhum "the Cuillins of Rhum". Whether this is an old name or not I cannot say, but I leave readers to draw their own conclusions. A Danish gentlemanI once met suggested that the name might be old Norse – a not improbable theory – Kjölen being, he said, high rocks, also descriptive of the range.

'The particularized names of peaks, corries, bealachs, etc., may be divided into several different classes: 1st, the old undisputed names, most of which are in the 6-inch Ordnance Survey maps; 2nd, the old names with disputed variations; and 3rd, the new "convenience" names of quite recent application.

'To begin with Class 1. – Starting the ridge at Sgurr na h-Uamha, Sgurr nan Gillean, Sgurr a' Bhasteir, Bruach na Frithe, Bidein Druim nan Ramh, Sgurr Thuilm, Sgurr Ghreadaidh, An Diallaid,

Sgurr nan Gobhar, Sgurr Dearg, Sgurr Sgumain, Sgurr Dubh, Sgurr Dubh na Da Bheinn, Sgurr nan Eag, and Gars-Bheinn. These are all, so far as I know, undisputed as regard form on the Glen Brittle side. There are, however, different readings of their meaning in some instances, Sgurr nan Gillean, for instance. It is usually translated, "peak of the young men", from some idea of the enormous death-roll caused by mythical attempts to ascend it! Mr. Mackenzie of the Crofter Commission, whom I had the pleasure of meeting once at Broadford, gave a mixed Gaelic-Norse meaning to this striking peak, and one, too, fully borne out by the topographical facts, i.e. the "peak of the ghylls or gullies". There are a good many places in the North-Western Highlands, in Skye and Harris, for instance, among others, where gill (as it is written on the Ordnance Survey 6-inch maps) forms either the beginning or end of a name, Buabisgill, Vikisgill, to take two in the immediate neighbourhood of the peak, both "ghylls" as they would be called in the lake country. I think this bears out Mr. MacKenzie's contention that the name is given from the deep "ghylls" dividing the pinnacles.

'Sgurr a' Ghreadaidh (as written in Ordnance Survey maps) is another name of doubtful meaning. As far as I can gather from dictionaries, its Gaelic meaning in English is "peak of thrashings or rushing wind". This name might with equal justice be applied to every peak and corrie in the range. Was not a camping party's tent during my stay at Brittle blown into the air in Coire Lagan? Professor W. P. Ker scouted this translation, and held by the old Norsk, Greta, "clear waters". This translation of the name is quite exceptionally accurate in this case, for of all the clear streams in Skye, and they are more than usually clear, the Greta is the clearest, and the springs in Coire a' Ghreadaidh (Ordnance Survey spelling) are more numerous than any of the other corries, certainly on the Brittle side. The peak also discharges a great deal of water into Coruisk, a very watery place, as its name, Coir-uisg, signifies.

'The old names, that either do not appear on the Ordnance Survey maps, or about which there are differences of opinion, are Sgurr Beag or Sgurr an Fhithich, Sgurr Dubh a' Bhasteir – the savage rock at the head of Am Basteir corrie – Sgurr na Banachdich, or as some natives call it, Sgurr na Bannachaig. This latter name has been a source of considerable discussion. The first rendering, 'Smallpox peak', is not only repulsive, but on consideration, unlikely. It is supposed to be given to the peak from red spots (say some) on the rocks; others say from rounded pits in the rock. I am not clear where the red spots are, but the rounded pits appear wherever the peridotite rock is *in situ*, and it is mostly so at head of Coir' a' Ghrunnda and in Garbh-choire. In any case the name of the peak is probably older than the occurrence of smallpox in Skye. It is a fact, however, that the greater number of the inhabitants, including one of the oldest shepherds, call it Sgurr na Banachdich. Against this is the fact that there are the rough remains of two shielings in Coire na Banachdich, which means that the cows were driven there to feed in summer, and these occur too – less obviously seen, however – in Coir' a' Ghreadaidh. Bannachaig means "Milkmaid", i.e. "Coire of the milkmaid", not only a more agreeable name, but much more likely to be the true one.

'The name Sgurr Coire an Lochan (given by Professor Collie and myself, to distinguish the peak then unnamed) is on inquiry found to be known to the shepherds at Brittle as Sgurr Dubh a' Choire Lochan.

'Probably Sgurr Alasdair was the first of the new names – so called, as most climbers know, from the late Sheriff Alexander Nicolson, who made the first ascent. Knight's Peak, the large pinnacle of Sgurr nan Gillean, and Sgurr Mhic Choinnich, were the next. The name, Knight's Peak, arose from the first ascent made by Professor Knight, then of St. Andrews. It does not appear on any map, and is difficult to render into Gaelic. Sgurr Mhic Choinnich is the Gaelic for Pic Mhic Choinnich, as it was first called by Mr. Charles Pilkington, after John Mackenzie. These names date back to the early eighties of last century. As climbing increased, more names were added, but it was the advent of Professor Harker and the Geological Survey that was the cause of the remainder, with an exception or two. These exceptions are the famous a' Chioch, an inspiration of John Mackenzie's in 1906, the day after its first ascent by Professor Collie and himself. The other is the peak Sgurr na Calleag (old woman). This is the point on the ridge below the "Inaccessible". John Mackenzie and a lady he was climbing with are responsible for this. The Ordnance Survey map has An Stac on this, but John says he believes this ought to apply to the "Inaccessible", or Old Man of Skye, as it also has been called. Certainly An Stac is rather more appropriate to the pinnacle than to the other, which, though it has a striking appearance from certain parts of the Cuillin, is not really a very marked peak.

'Professor Harker named Sgurr na Bhairnich and An Caisteal (not on Ordnance Survey), peaks to the west of Bruach na Frithe, and his help in other names was invaluable. Professor Collie and Mr. Naismith named, or helped to name, others. These are Sgurr an Fheadain, Sgurr Thormaid (after Professor Collie), Sgurr Thearlaich (after Mr. Charles Pilkington), I cannot recall who suggested this, but it is most just and appropriate; Sgurr Coire an Lochan (as on Ordnance Survey), or Sgurr Dubh a' Choire Lochan (by the natives); Sgurr Dubh Beag, and Sgurr a' Choire Bhig. Sron na Ciche was given at the time the Cioch was named, and distinguishes the massive shoulder of Sgurr Sgumain, on the side of which the Cioch stands. The lower ridges to the east of Coiruisg and south of Harta Corrie are all old names, i.e. Druim nan Ramh, Druim Hain, Sgurr Hain, Meall Dearg, and Sgurr na Stri.

'About the names of the corries there is less difference of opinion than about the peaks; however, there is one important exception, that is whether the Ordnance Survey map has not reversed the position of the names Coir a' Mhadaidh and Tairneilear. John Mackenzie holds that they have, and certainly it is odd that Sgurr a' Mhadaidh stands at the head (according to Ordnance Survey) of the Tairneilear, and not at the head of Coir a' Mhadaidh.

It is interesting to note that in 1968 the Ordnance Survey conceded their long held error, and Coir a' Mhadaidh is now under Sgurr a' Mhadaidh.

'The names of the passes over the ridge are not all given on the maps; those that are, correspond with the native nomenclature. The shepherds at Brittle call the gap between Sgurr Dearg and Sgurr Mhic Choinnich, Bealach a' Choire Lagan; and the col between Sgurr Thearlaich and Sgurr Dubh na Da Bheinn, Bealach Coir' an Lochain. For convenience sake, the top of the stone shoot between Sron na Ciche and Sgurr Sgumain has been called Bealach Coir' a' Ghrunnda; and the sharp gap between Sgurr Mhic Choinnich and Sgurr Thearlaich, Bealach Mhic Choinnich – the natives are not responsible for these.

'There is considerable doubt as to the true position of An Dorus, at the head of Coir' a' Ghreadaidh. John Mackenzie holds that it is not the obvious gap at the foot of Sgurr a' Mhadaidh as given in Ordnance Survey, but the deep cut a little further up the ridge of Sgurr a' Ghreadaidh. It may be mentioned here that Mr. Campbell at Glen Brittle always calls the neck of the pass at Bealach Core na

Banachdich, An Dorus; not that this means that the other is not also An Dorus, as it is really the most important of the two, and is known by that name in Glen Brittle.

'The second edition of the Ordnance Survey 6-inch maps has altered the name Meall a' Mhaim, the hump north of the Mam, to Am Mam, and still calls the pass itself Bealach a' Mhaim. John Mackenzie always calls it – the pass – Am Mam. I don't understand why they made this alteration. They also print the name Tobar nan Uaislean, on the long shoulder of Bruach na Frithe. The natives call the big spring at the top of the Mam, Tobar nan Uaislean, "the gentleman's well". In Glen Brittle we call the shoulder Sron nan Tobair for convenience. There are a great many local names along the lower slopes omitted on the Ordnance Survey, the maps in different parts of the Highlands being very unequal in this respect, some very full and others very empty.'

Flora

ALF SLACK

Each of the six fingers of Skye areas have characteristics which are reflected in the plants, and for the purpose of description it is convenient to take each in turn without necessarily being too strict in drawing boundaries between them:

In MINGINISH the rough gabbro of the Black Cuillin provides so many crags at a high altitude, and the rock itself is of such a basic nature chemically, that one might expect to find a great variety of arctic and alpine plants on this range, but, on the other hand, the rock is well known for its stability, and in fact it weathers down too slowly to produce a soil such as would support the growth of many plants. Moreover, the relatively high rainfall flushes away what little soil tends to form. Thus it will be realized that the Black Cuillin is not very distinguished for its mountain plants. Nevertheless, the following may be seen in the course of an ascent, roughly in the order given, which is also roughly the order of increasing rarity. The Alpine Ladies Mantle (*Alchemilla alpina*) covers scree edges and is often washed down by streams to low levels where it survives well beside burns. The Starry Saxifrage (*Saxifraga stellaris*) is washed down to a less extent, but begins to be seen in rocky corners by torrents from about 1000 ft., becoming commoner at higher levels. The Kidney Sorrel (*Oxyria digyna*) is like-wise liable to be seen washed down, but is most at home in wet gullies above 2000 ft. The Purple Saxifrage (*Saxifraga oppositifolia*) festoons damp rocks with its trailing small-leaved branches which produce vivid purple flowers soon after the snow melts. The Least Cudweed (*Gnaphalium supinum*) selects areas of stabilized scree close to the summit ridge and with it may grow the Creeping Sibbaldia (*Sibbaldia procumbens*) with its grey-green trefoil leaves and insignificant yellow flowers. This last is surprisingly rare in the Cuillin though common in other parts of Skye. Finally, on the summits themselves may be found the Least Willow (*Salix herbacea*), each branch of which bears only two rounded leaves used to being crushed by the unwitting climbers' boots. Another plant of the summits is the very characteristic Wooly Fringed Moss (*Rhacomitrium lanuginosun*), which may cover acres on the flatter tops such as Bruach na Frithe. Growing with it is the Rigid Sedge (*Carex bigelowii*), the spiked Woodrush (*Luzula spicata*) and the Highland Rush (*Juncus trifidus*), the latter never still in the slightest breeze.

All of these mentioned so far may be matched on many a mainland peak, but we come now to some plants a little more characteristic of the western peaks in Scotland. The Alpine Saussurea (*Saussurea alpina*), named after the famous alpinist, is abundant in the Black Cuillin. Its purple, thistle-like flowers are produced in August. It is widespread also on mainland peaks but more particularly on western ones. The Northern Rock-cress (*Cardaminopsis petraea*) is even more a western hill plant, occurring for example in Ben Lui, Ben Nevis, Liathach and Ben Hope. It is abundant in the Black Cuillin, possibly more so than on any other range of similar size. While on the summits some other plants may be seen such as the Moss Campion (*Silene acaulis*) and the mountain form of the Thrift (*Ameria maritima*). These show the cushion habit so often adopted by plants subjected to strong winds. Another plant of the summits is the Trailing Azalea (*Loiseleuria procumbens*) which is more likely near bealachs or on shoulders provided there is some flattish stony ground. In the Black Cuillins there are few places suitable for it.

On the descent from the summits some further plants may be seen, particularly if a route is followed between the bottom of a steep crag and the top of a scree shoot. On the rocks may occur the Alpine Clubmoss (*Lycopodium alpinum*) with light yellow upstanding cones if it is in fruiting condition, and other Clubmosses are also to be expected. The Fir Club-moss (*Lycopodium selago*) is abundant from the highest levels to quite low ones but the Stags Horn Clubmoss (*Lycopodium clavatum*) is unlikely at the higher levels and is not a rock-dweller, occurring here and there amongst heather on the moors. The Northern Bedstraw (*Galium boreale*) grows from cracks in the rocks and has a distinctive arrangement of its leaves – four at each node. The mountain form of Juniper (*Juniperus communis*) hangs from cracks in the rocks or spreads horizontally over slabs, differing markedly from the lowland form of the same plant which stands erect as a small bush familiar to many mountaineers in Rothiemurchus. The Rock Bramble (*Rubus saxatilis*) grows from cracks in the rock, and has long runners like those of a strawberry by means of which it spreads. The red fruit containing only two or three drupes is not very often produced. The Rose-root (*Sedum rosea*) with smooth greyish leaves slightly reminiscent of a diminutive cabbage is a 'dual purpose' plant found on mountain crags and sea-shore cliffs. There are a number of other plants with a similar dual role including the Thrift already mentioned. The Goldenrod (*Solidago virgaurea*) is a very common crag plant. Its yellow flower-heads tend to be larger at higher altitudes but fewer in number, and there is a variety to be seen sometimes on the summits with large flower-heads on very short stalks. Much less common on the crags is the Globe Flower (*Trollius europaeus*) which selects rather damp places. Also uncommon and rather addicted to overhangs is the Holly Fern (*Polystichun lonchitis*). Under overhangs also, a lucky search may reveal the Alpine Saxifrage (*Saxifraga nivalis*) which bears a resemblance to the Starry Saxifrage but has its whitish flowers more clustered at the head of a hairy stalk. From the rock, or from the scree below may spring the fronds of the Parsley Fern (*Cryptogramma crispa*) which greatly resembles the potherb after which it is named. Last to be mentioned is the great rarity of the Cuillins, the Alpine Rockcress (*Arabis alpina*) which is found in a few Cuillin coires in rather inaccessible positions and nowhere else in Britain. Its white flowers are produced in July. There are many more plants which the mountaineer may encounter in the Cuillins, but this account must not degenerate into a mere list and some of them are more characteristic of other parts which we now turn.

First, without leaving Minginish we should examine the lowland flora, for in addition to the Cuillins, Minginish boasts large areas of moorland, both grass moor and heather moor. It also has some interesting lochans, and beside the sea there is impressive sea-cliff, some salt-marsh and a little sand. Of woodland there is virtually none save the forestry plantations which are always unpromising areas for botanical variety, and of cultivated land with its characteristic crops and weeds again there is only a small area.

Heather moor is very largely occupied by the three common heathers, *Culluna vulgaris* the Ling Heather, *Erica cinerea*, the Fine-leaved Heath with its dark bell-flowers, and *Erica tetralix* the Cross-leaved Heath with its pale bell-flowers. Of these, the first is usually dominant, with the dark bell-heather sharing the drier rockier areas, and the pale-bell heather sharing the wetter peaty areas. Beneath and between these shrubby heathers grows a characteristic selection of acid-soil tolerating herbs. These include the Heath Bedstraw (*Galium saxatile*) with small white flowers, the Lousewort (*Pedicularis sylvatica*) with pink flowers having a prominently arched upper lip, the Milkwort (*Polygala serpyllifolia*), with blue, pink or white flowers and intricate petals, and the Heath Orchid (*Dactylorchis maculata*) with beautiful white or pink-spotted flowers and black-spotted leaves. Where the soil is less acid, as it is over large areas in Minginish owing to the presence of much basalt, grass moor replaces heather moor. The Blue Moor Grass (*Molinia caerulea*) occupies large areas and can give rise to very irregular tufts which may make walking difficult and even dangerous. The Tufted Hair-grass (*Deschampsia caespitosa*) is usually present too and it can produce even worse tufts. This grass may be recognized by the roughness of the leaves when drawn backwards through the fingers. These tuft-forming grasses are large and grow on the wetter moors, but much pleasanter walking is provided by the smaller grasses such as the Sweet Vernal Grass (*Anthoxanthum odoratum*), which many like to chew, the Mat-grass (*Nardus stricta*), and the Fescues (of the genus *Festuca*), which provide the very fine-leaved grasses of many hill-slopes, and others. Pleasant grassy walking is however more a factor of grazing than of the type of grass, for on some of the small un-grazed islands off the coast of Skye fescues grow to enormous lengths and one sinks deep at every step.

With the grasses grow another characteristic set of associates. In the wetter areas the Bog Myrtle (*Myrica gale*) grows widely and imparts its very pleasant scent to the air as boots bruise its leaves. Some small willows may be seen, particularly the Eared Sallow (*Salix aurita*), with its notably crinkled leaves, and the Creeping Willow (*Salix repens*). In the drier parts, Thyme (*Thymus drucei*) and Fairy

1. Loch Coruisk, evening.

2. Sgurr nan Gillean. The pinnacle ridge in winter seen from Sgurr a'Bhasteir.

Flax (*Linum catharticum*) are abundant. Daisies (*Bellis perennis*) and Dandelions (Species of *Taraxacum*) occur but sparingly. Much more frequent are the Cats-ear (*Hypochaeris radicata*) in the spring, and the Hawkbit (*Leontodon autumnalis*) in the autumn which are liable to be taken for Dandelions but lack the hollow stem. So far, the description of the moors of Minginish could apply to anywhere, on the mainland of Scotland, but it is in the flushes on the moors that the plants characteristic of the West of the country most manifest themselves. In these areas, where moisture oozes as one puts one's weight on the soil, or where a trickle begins to form itself into the forerunner of a burn, one may find the Black Bog-rush (*Schoenus nigricans*) and the White Beak-rush (*Rhyncospora alba*). There will be some Narrow-leaved Cotton-grass (*Eriophorum angustifolium*) and quite possibly the Broad-leaved (*Eriophorum latifolium*) which is rare in general but quite common in Skye. There will be insectivorous plants if as is usual the soil is peaty. The Round-leaved Sundew (*Drosera rotundifolia*) is the commonest, but the Long-leaved (*Drosera anglica*) is quite abundant. The common Butterwort (*Pinguicula vulgaris*) abounds, and here and there the Pale Butterwort (*Pinguicula lusitannica*) will be seen. Another insectivorous plant, the Bladderwort (*Utricularia minor*) is really a plant of the lochs, but it does occur in damp places on the hillside.

There are several small fresh water lochans in Minginish and two large ones, Loch Coruisk and Loch na Creitheach. All can be treated as peaty lochs containing rather base-poor water. As a rule they have a stony edge, and frequently stones lie on the bottom, but in places their edges consist of peaty banks and their bottoms of black peat. Round the shallow edge of such a loch is developed a zone of emergent vegetation. Rushes (*Juncus effusus*) and Horse-tails (*Equisetum fluviatile*) are common but this zone is not as well represented as in bodies of water richer in bases. The Lesser Spear-wort (*Ranunculus flammula*) often forms most of this zone, giving a yellow edge to the lochan when it is in flower. A little deeper into the lochan brings us to the zone of submerged leaves, and here the characteristic plants are the Water Lobelia (*Lobelia dortmana*), with pale blue flowers on an emerging stalk, and the Quillwort (*Isoetes lacustris*), a strange relation of the ferns with leaves like twisted spines. In this zone too should be counted the Shore-weed (*Littorella lacustris*) which, though a flowering plant, looks like a small quillwort. A Skye speciality also falls in this zone, the Pipewort (*Eriocaulon septan-*

gulare). It has a strange world distribution being found widely in North America but nowhere on this side of the Atlantic except W. Ireland, Skye and Colonsay. In the deeper parts of the lochs only vegetation with floating leaves can survive. This includes the White Water-lily (*Nymphaea alba*), the Yellow Water-lily (*Nuphar lutea*), the Potamogetons (Pond-weeds) and the Sparganiums, of which *Sparganium angustifolium* with its long thin leaves may most often be seen.

So much for the landward areas in Minginish. Turning to the sea-coasts, the majority of Skye mountaineers must have been impressed by the steep cliffs rising many hundreds of feet at a high angle such as may be seen to the west of Loch Brittle. Common maritime species occur here such as the Thrift (*Armeria maritima*), the Sea campion (*Silene maritima*), and the English Stone-crop (*Sedum anglica*), along with rock species such as the Rose root (*Sedum rosea*), and the Stone-bramble (*Rubus saxatilis*) already encountered high in the Cuillins. Some plants of the woodlands find shady conditions on northern slopes, in gullies, or amongst bushes of Hazel (*Corylus avellana*), Holly (*Ilex aquifolia*), and Aspen (*Populus tremula*). These woodland forms include the Red Campion (*Silene dioica*), the Bluebell (*Endymion non-scriptus*), the Wood Sorrell (*Oxalis acetosella*) and rather more locally the Wood Vetch (*Vicia sylvatica*) with its feathery foliage clinging by tendrils, and pale blue and white flowers. Here and there some rarer plants of the open cliff may be found including the Carline Thistle (*Carlina vulgaris*) with its striking yellowish flowers, the Biting Stonecrop (*Sedum acre*) also with yellow flowers, the Bitter Vetch (*Vicia orobus*) and the Red Broomrape (*Orobanche alba*), the last growing parasitically on Thyme (*Thymus drucei*), which is abundant. The flora of these cliffs is very varied and interesting and may well repay further exploration. Before leaving them mention should be made of four plants which occur in damp gullies or corners near sea-level here. The first is the Royal Fern (*Osmunda regalis*), formerly quite common on the western sea-board of Scotland but now much reduced in numbers owing to unscrupulous collection for horticulture. The second is another fern, the Sea Spleenwort (*Asplenium marinum*), whose succulent glossy fronds fill many a crack within reach of the salt spray. Thirdly, the Scottish Lovage (*Ligusticum scoticum*) is a Scottish coastal member of the parsley family with only slightly divided leaves which used to find favour for culinary purposes. The fourth plant is the Tutsan

(*Hypericum androsaemum*), with leaves like a rhododendron and large yellow flowers. It is a plant of western distribution.

Descending to sea-level and deserting the rocky outcrops we find a narrow zone of plants most characteristic of salt-marsh conditions. Several sedges and rushes occur in this zone particularly the Mud Rush (*Juncus gerardii*). More easily recognized plants include the Sea Milkwort (*Glaux maritina*), which at times produces a notable pink glow with its abundance of flowers, and the Scurvy-grass (*Cochlearia officinalis*) which has an extremely close relative (*Cochlearia alpina*) growing as an alpine plant on the mountains. Another pair of plants worth mentioning in this connection are the Arrow Grasses (*Triglochin*), one species growing in these salt-marsh conditions and another growing in fresh-water marsh conditions up to quite high levels in the hills. Thrift (*Armeria maritima*) is usually abundant in this narrow salt marsh zone which is astonishingly continuous round the coast being only interrupted by sheer cliff, as at exposed headland and by patches of sand. In places, particularly at the head of the inlets in which Skye is so rich this salt marsh extends to cover wide areas, but the number of species represented in it is comparatively small.

The patches of sea-shore sand in Minginish (or anywhere in Skye) are few, the strand at Loch Brittle being rather unique. It is not surprising therefore that few plants characteristic of this kind of habitat occur, the most striking one being the Sea Rocket (*Cakile maritima*) at Glen Brittle.

Behind the sea-shore sand or salt marsh zone, a zone of fresh water marsh frequently occurs dominated as a rule by the Yellow Flag (*Iris psuedacorus*). The edge of this zone may be manured by sea-weed washed up at exceptionally high tides and nitrophilous plants occur here, such as the Stinging Nettle (*Urtica diocia*) and the Skull-cap (*Scutellaria galericulata*). A plant to be found here and there on the landward side of this zone is the Marsh Pimpernel (*Anagallis tenella*) which though not confined to the west coast in Britain is very much more abundant there than elsewhere. Its relatively large pale pink flowers arising from a diminutive creeping leafy stem are very striking.

TROTTERNISH has a high level spine from Beinn a Chearcaill to the Quirang. The altitudes throughout are about 2000 feet, but there is a great deal of steep rock, and as the basalt of which this spine is composed breaks down more readily than gabbro into a soil there is much more vegetation on the ledges, and therefore this is the region in Skye which is richest in arctic and alpine plants. All the Cuillin plants occur here except the Alpine Rock-Cress (*Arabis alpina*) and in addition there are several arctic and alpine plants not seen elsewhere in Skye. The Alpine Pearlwort (*Sagina saginoides*) which occasionally can produce a carpet of thousands of small white starry flowers is one. The Mossy Cyphal (*Cherleria sedoides*) with rather insignificant yellow-green flowers is another, the Mossy Saxifrage (*Saxifraga hyponides*) is a third and there are several others of a rather insignificant nature. At the northern end of the spine however, a striking plant is to be found, the Mountain Avens (*Dryas octopetala*). It has peculiar oak-shaped leaves with a white undersurface due to abundant hairs and striking eight-petalled white flowers. It grows in Britain only on rocky soils rich in lime and usually at an altitude of about 2000 ft., though often lower on the north and west side of the country and higher towards the east. One further speciality of the Trotternish spine must be mentioned. *Koenigia islandica*, a small plant with no common name was discovered here for the first time in Britain only a few years ago. It is circumpolar in distribution and in Trotternish occurs on semi-stable fine screes at altitudes of about 2000 ft. It has since been found in Mull but not elsewhere in Britain.

The moors, lochs, sea-cliffs and shore line of Trotternish in general resemble the descriptions given above for Minginish and need not be elaborated here. Portree Harbour and Loch Snizort Beag are extensive inlets at the heads of which salt-marsh conditions prevail. Along much of the East coast and part of the West steep sea-cliffs fringe the peninsula. There are two large lochs and some small ones.

Turning our attention to VATTERNISH, we find a region of lowland by comparison with the previous two areas. There is a central ridge, but it rises to 1000 ft. but seldom and rocky outcrops are scattered and small. Cultivation is more widespread though very piecemeal, and one cannot but notice the prevalence of the two north western weeds of cultivation, Corn Marigold (*Chrysanthemum segetum*) with its golden yellow flowers and rather waxy looking leaves, and the Corn Spurrey (*Spergularia arvensis*), which when well grown gives a revolting odour to the entire field. The moors, which are most extensive in this area, repeat the features described for Minginish, but where the basalt is near the sufrace with little or no peat covering it, a rather attractive meadow type of herbage may result. With bed-rock close to the surface short fescue and other grasses spread from the moors with attendant Thyme (*Thymus drucei*), Lousewort (*Pedicularis sylvatica*), Fairy Flax (*Linum cathcarticum*) and Birds Foot Trefoil (*Lotus corniculatus*). The Thyme provides an attractive scent and the yellow, white and red flowers of this mixture provide a pleasing appearance. Orchids frequently invade this grassland. In the driest areas the White Mountain Orchid (*Leucorchis albida*) occurs rather sparingly. The deliciously scented pink Fragrant Orchids (*Gymnadenia conopsea*) on the other hand are more often colonial and may occur in thousands in a good year. In the wetter areas of deeper soil and longer grass Butterfly Orchids (species of *Platanthera*) may occur, though, as with all orchids, they are subject to extraordinary changes in abundance from year to year. In the wettest meadows of this type the Dwarf Purple Orchid (*Dactylorchis purpurella*) makes a marked contribution with its brilliant spikes of purple flowers peeping through the grass. Another orchid, the Early Marsh Orchid (*Dactylorchis incarnata*) is less commonly seen with its shorter flesh-coloured spikes.

DUNVEGAN. In a way this area is comparable with the Arnaval area. It is convenient to treat Arnaval between Lochs Eynort and Harport, together with Dunvegan. The islands of Loch Bracadale (Wiay, Tarner, etc.), may be regarded as being the tops of the submerged ridge. The outstanding feature of this area is its impressive sea-cliff scenery. In three places cliffs rise nearly 1000 ft. directly from the sea. The sea-cliff plants mentioned for Minginish occur along this coast and in addition some arctic and alpine types inhabit ledges on these cliffs. Amongst these, the Moss Campion (*Silene acaulis*) may be mentioned as occupying considerable areas in suitable places. The Alpine Saussurea (*Saussurea alpina*) is another species occasionally present, and the Hoary Whitlow Grass (*Draba incana*) is also to be found. The Fir Clubmoss (*Lycopodium selago*) and the Northern Bedstraw (*Galium boreale*) occur together with two saxifrages, the Mossy Saxifrage (*Saxifraga hypnoides*) with white flowers and the Purple Saxifrage (*Saxifraga oppositifolia*). The most fascinating arctic-alpine plant however is the Mountain Avens (*Dryas octopetala*) growing here in small quantity at a low elevation facing the full fury of the Atlantic gales. It occupies similar habitats in Mull, Kintyre and in the West of Ireland.

Inland the Arnaval, Healaval area compares closely with neighbouring Vatternish and even Healaval Beg rising to 1601 ft. has few cliffs to support an upland vegetation.

SLEAT. This, the most eastern and southern part of Skye, is also the most sheltered from the Atlantic storms and in consequence woodland plays a large part here than elsewhere in the island. Woodlands of some extent occur to the east of Kyleakin overlooking Loch Alsh, around Isle Ornsay, Near Ord on Loch Eishort, south of Tarskavaig, and near Armadale. Most of these woods are Birchwood (*Betula pubescens*) with some Oak (*Quercus petraea*) and Hazel (*Corylus avellana*), which predominates locally. Ash (*Fraxinus exelsior*) is represented in some areas and other trees and bushes contribute such as Pine (*Pinus sylvestris*), Aspen (*Populus tremula*), Elder (*Sambucus nigra*), Hawthorn (*Crataegus monagyna*). Beside streams Alder (*Alnus glutinosa*) is the rule. Honeysuckle (*Lonicera periclymum*) climbs on the trees particularly in rocky woods, and Ivy (*Hedera helix*) and Holly (*Ilex aquifolia*) occur sporadically. The ground flora includes little of special interest, the usual woodland plants of rather wet woods being present such as Wood Anemone (*Anemone nemorosa*), Bugle (*Ajuga reptans*), Woodrush (*Luzula sylvatica*), Red Campion (*Silene dioica*), Yellow Pimpernel (*Lysimachia nemorum*), Angelica (*Angelica sylvatica*). In the areas with a better soil, as around Ord, Ransoms (*Allium ursinum*) and Woodruff (*Asperula odorata*) occur and give their characteristic scents to the air. The Armadale woods include planted Beech (*Fagus sylvatica*) and in this area occurs a rare orchid, the Sword-leaved Helleborine (*cephalanthera longifolia*) which is thinly distributed on the West Coast of Scotland and makes here its one excursion in to the Hebrides.

Of Sleat's moors and lochs the remarks made for Minginish apply. There are no markedly high sea-cliffs but rocky shores, salt-marsh and gravelly beaches provide the usual assemblage of maritime plants. There remain however two areas in Sleat worth special mention. One is the mountainous part to the east of Kyleakin which has two fairly high hills, Sgurr na Coinnich (2401 ft.) and Ben Aslak (1984 ft.). As the rock is of Torridonion sandstone the vegetation is of comparatively little interest. Some arctic and alpine plants appear such as the Alpine Ladies Mantle (*Alchemilla alpina*) the Alpine Clubmoss (*Lycopodium alpinum*), Thrift (*Armeria maritima*) as a summit plant, the Least Cudweed (*Gnaphalium supinum*), Juniper (*Juniperus communis*), Least Willow (*Salix herbacea*), Starry Saxifrage (*Saxifraga stellaris*) etc. If there were corries of a rocky nature this might well prove to be quite an interesting area, but the rocky outcrops are on the whole small so that sheep and deer limit the vegetation to such plants as can withstand cropping. The other special area of Sleat is the limestone area around Ord. Here the Cambrian limestone comes to the surface over a considerable area and produces a fascinating pattern of limestone pavement with numerous grikes. In the grikes a variety of lime-loving plants can be found, amongst which small ferns are prominent, such as the Maidenhair Spleenwort (*Asplenium trichomanes*), the Wall-rue (*Ssplenium ruta-muraria*), the Bladder Fern (*Cystopteris fragilis*), and the Harts-tongue (*Phyllitis scolopendrium*). With these may be found also some herbs with delicate foliage such as Herb Robert (*Geranium robertianum*) and Enchanters Nightshade (*Circaea intermedia*). The abundant lime makes any nitrogen present freely available, so that in selected spots nitrophilous plants such as stinging nettles (*Urtica dioica*), and Chickweed (*Stellaria media*) thrive. On the more exposed limestone ridges plants with rather leathery leaves are more common such as Thyme (*Thymus drucei*), Creeping Willow (*Salix repens*) and some grasses such as Blue Moor Grass (*Molinia caerulea*), as much at home here as on the moors, and the Hairy Oat (*Avena pubescens*). The Centaury (*Centaurium minus*) adds its beautiful pink flowers in small quantities as does the Hairy rock-cress (*Arabis hirsuta*) its white ones. Much of the limestone is wooded with Hazel growing from the grikes and an abundance of mosses on the boulders.

STRATHAIRD, for convenience, is taken to include also the area South of Broadford dominated by Ben Suardal (922 ft.). Though this area is of relatively low relief compared with the adjacent Red and Black Cuillin, it is an area of great interest to botanists and has been a centre of pilgrimage since Martin Martin in 1703 included a reference to it in his 'Description of the Western Isles of Scotland'. The reason for its extraordinary vegetation lies in the many square miles where the surface is composed of Cambrian Limestone, producing the same pattern of grikes and pavements which were noted near Ord, only here on a much larger scale. In addition to the plants noted near Ord other more decided lime-loving plants appear. The Green Spleenwort (*Asplenium viride*), which is more characteristic of higher zones as a rule replaces other spleenworts in some of the grikes. Mountain Avens (*Dryas octopetala*) here is present in great abundance from near road level to the summit of Ben Suardal. The Dark Red Helleborine (*Epipactis atrorubens*) is an orchid which springs from grikes and also from vertical cliffs over a wide area here. Another orchid with green flowers is the Twayblade (*Listera ovata*).

The Red Broomrape (*Orobanche alba*), which was noted on sea-cliffs in Minginish and other areas also occurs inland here springing from vertical limestone rocks near the Thyme on which it is parasitic. Apart from the Cambrian Limestone area, Strathaird includes areas of Jurassic limestones and other rocks which have some interesting features, but nothing differing sufficiently from areas already mentioned to justify any detailed description.

To summarize, the Island of Skye is seen to contain a great variety of habitats from the wet acid peaty loch-edges to the dry calcareous limestone pavements, and from the flat lowland salt-marshes to the steep elevated crags. In consequence it has a varied flora of some 300 relatively common flowering plants and ferns and a fair selection of less common ones. Notable for their absence are the common roadside and woodland plants of the south such as the Cuckoo-pint (*Arum macultum*) and Hedge-parsley (*Anthriscus sylvestris*). By compensation the flora includes many exclusively or predominantly Atlantic species such as the Dwarf Purple Orchid (*Orchis purpurella*) and the Marsh Pimpernel (*Anagallis tenella*). Marsh plants are well represented as is to be expected in a 'misty isle' and by contrast many plants characteristic of drier areas are absent or extremely rare. This applies for instance to the hairy annuals or biennials such as the Mullein (*Verbascum thapsus*) and to some small Legumes such as the Birds Foot (*Ornithopus perpusillus*) and ephemerals like the Whitlow Grass (*Erophila verna*). The rarity of these latter types draws attention to the great predominance of perennial forms, which is undoubtedly an adaptation to the climate of Skye, with its unreliable summers giving little opportunity for annuals to establish themselves from seed, but allowing the perennials, once established, to increase their hold. This same climate places a premium on the storage of plant food in creeping or underground stems and roots, and by the spread of these, plants of considerable rarity may become locally common. The Stags Horn Clubmoss (*Lycopodium clavatum*) illustrates this point well.

The arctic and alpine plants in particular have to grow during the even shorter cooler summers of the mountains, so that they are nearly all perennials, with various adaptations for vegetative spread to supplement the unreliable seed-production. Further they often show adaptations for lessening the trials of wind, rain or drought. The hairy undersurface of the Saussurea for instance traps still air next to the leaf, and the curled-back leaf of the Trailing Azalea prevents direct evaporation from the undersurface. Drought is a real danger in spite of the rainfall owing to the rapidity of the drainage on steep high slopes.

Apart from the arctic and alpine plants of Skye, the plants of the wet moorlands, of the sea-cliffs and of the Cambrian limestone areas are the three most outstanding floras. They contain few or no plants of exceptional rarity, though quite a few of limited distribution, but they contain many plants decidedly western in their British distribution and often in numbers rarely seen on the adjacent mainland.

Naturally it is with the adjacent mainland and with other nearby islands that one makes comparisons, and Skye fares reasonably well in such comparisons. Of the arctic and alpine plants there are a few of quite frequent occurrence in nearby Ross and Inverness not represented in Skye. Such is the knotted clubmoss (*Lycopodium annotinum*) yet to be recorded for Skye. Its absence is a reminder that the flora of islands is usually an impoverished version of that of the nearest mainland. On the other hand the Alpine Rock-cress (*Arabis alpina*) and the *Koenigia islandica* represent an improvement on Ross and Inverness. Other islands of the inner Hebrides also have specialities of this sort, particularly, Rhum and Raasay. Similar remarks apply with regard to the wetter moors and lochans, where another club-moss, *Lycopodium inundatum*, provides an example of a plant locally abundant on the mainland but absent from Skye, whereas the Pipewort (*Eriocaulon septangulare*) represents Skye's improvement on the mainland flora. For comparison with Skye's limestone flora, Kishorn on the mainland provides a close parallel not fully appreciated till recently. Raasay has a somewhat different assemblage of plants developed on Jurassic limestone. Skye's sea-cliffs however are almost unique in this part of Scotland. Cliffs there are on the adjacent mainland, but they lack the height or the steepness of Waterstein Head or Dunvegan Head and hence support only some of the plants and there in much lesser numbers. Rassay and Rhum again compete with Skye each with some impressive cliffs and in addition Canna and Eigg have cliffs of note. The Carline Thistle (*Carlina vulgaris*) grows on all these islands but not on the mainland. The red broomrape (*Orobanche alba*) is on Raasay and Canna, as well as on a few mainland cliffs, the Bitter Vetch (*Vicia orobus*) occur on Canna and Muck as well as occasionally on the mainland.

In these notes little or no reference has been made to plants other than flowering plants and ferns. The mosses, lichens, fungi and algae of Skye would each provide material for a similar account which it is hoped some one may be persuaded to put together in the not too distant future.

Bus and Walk

Skye is well served by bus services, and its mountains provide a fascinating variety of mountain ways. The linking of bus/boat services with hill traverses offer the best way of all of enjoying the opportunities. Up to date time tables may be obtained from the Skye Tourist Association office in Portree or Broadford, or from the Highlands and Islands Development Board, Castle Wynd, Inverness. Some recommended traverses that involve no climbing are listed below.

SLEAT:
Chapter 1 Bealach Udal in Kylerhea glen to Kyleakin over Sgurr na Coinnich.

STRATHAIRD:
Chapter 2:2. Head of Loch Slapin to the head of Loch Ainort over the col between Glas Bheinn Mor and Belig. Can be coupled to the ascent of either.
   3. Kilmairie to Camusunary – Elgol. (low level)
   4. Camusunary – Sligachan. (low level)
Chapter 3:5. Camusunary – Loch Coruisk or vice versa, coupled with boat to or from Elgol.
   Note: There is the short 'Bad Step'.
   6. Coruisk – Loch-a-Choire Riabbhach – Glen Sligachan.

CUILLIN:
   7. Coruisk-Bealach a' Garbh Coire – Coire a' Ghrunnda – Bealach a' Ghrunnda – Coire Lagan – Glen Brittle.
   8. Coruisk – Bealach na Banachdich – Glen Brittle.
   9. Coruisk – Glen Brittle by coast (one difficult section) (low level)
   10. Sligachan – Bruach na Frithe.
   11. Glen Brittle – Sgurr Alaisdair by stone shoot.

MINGINISH:
   12. Talisker – Preshal Mor – Preshal Beag – Glen Eynort.

BIBLIOGRAPHY

Much has been written on Skye, and an exhaustive list of books and magazine articles would fill too much space to allow of its being given here, but the following are of antiquarian interest as being written by many of the pioneers:—

A Summer in Skye, Alex. Smith, 1865.
The Hebrid Isles, R. W. Buchanan, new edition, 1883.
Rambles in Skye, Malcolm Ferguson, 1883.
History and Traditions of the Isle of Skye, Alex. Cameron, 1871.
The Misty Isle of Skye, J. A. MacCulloch, 1905.
Rock Climbing in Skye, Ashley P. Abraham, 1908.
British Mountain Climbs, George D. Abraham, 1909.
Mountain Adventures at Home and Abroad, George D. Abraham, 1910.
Autumns in Skye, Ross and Sutherland, Ratcliffe Barnet, John Grout, Edinburgh, 1946.
Cuillins of Skye, B. H. Humble, Robert Hale, 1952.
Alpine Journal—
Vol. XIII. *The Black Coolins*, C. Pilkington.
Vol. XV. *The Rocky Mountains of Skye*, Clinton Dent.
Vol. XXIII. *The Cuillin Hills*, G. Yeld.
Vol. XXVI. *A Week's Exploration on the Coolin*, J. M. A. Thomson.
Vol. XXXII. *The Island of Skye*, J. N. Collie.

Cairngorm Club Journal—
Vol. I. *Sgurr nan Gillean*, W. Tough.
  Hill Climbing in Skye, Prof. Adamson.
  Three Days in Skye, David Crombie.
  Sgurr Dearg and the Inaccessible Pinnacle, W. Tough.
Vol. V. *Skye with Cycle and Camera*, Alex. Simpson.
  On the Ridges of the Coolins, Wm. Barclay.
Vol. VI. *Midsummer in Glen Brittle*, H. C. Boyd.
  A Week's Climbing in Skye, J. R. Levack.
Vol. VII. *A Week at Sligachan*, J. R. Levack.
Vol. IX. *Fort William to Skye*, J. B. Nicol.
Vol. X. *A Rock-Climbing Novitiate in Skye*, A. M. M. Williamson.
  Climbing in Skye in Wet Weather, A. M. M. Williamson.

Climbers' Club Journal—
Vol. II. *A Fortnight in Skye*, R. E. T.
  A Walk over Blaven, E. A. Baker.
Vol. IX. *Camping in Skye*, A. and M. Gimson.
Vol. XII. *New Climbs in Coire Labain*, G. Barlow and H. B. Buckle.
  June Days in the Coolins, E. W. Steeple.
Vol. XIII. *The South-East Gully of Sgurr a' Mhadaidh*, E. W. Steeple.
Vol. I. (New Series, 1913.) *New Expeditions in the Coolin*, E. W.
  Steeple.

Journal of the Fell and Rock Climbing Club—
Vol. III. *Impressions of Skye*. J. Laycock.
  The Western Buttress of Sgurr Sgumain, A. E. Bagley.
Vol. IV. *Wandering in Skye*, E. W. Steeple.
Vol. V. *Climbing in the North-West Highlands*, T. H. Somervell.
  A Climbing Tour in the Highlands, G. S. Bower.

Rucksack Club Journal—
Vol. I. *In the Southern Cuillins*, A. G. Woodhead.
  A Day's Walk in Skye, A. E. Barker.
Vol. II. *A Week in Coire Ghreadaidh*, E. W. Steeple.
  A First Visit to Glen Brittle, W. Wallwork.
Vol. III. *Extracts from a Skye Diary*, W. Wallwork.
Vol. IV. *A New Climb on the Cioch*, H. R. C. C.
  On Skye, A. S. Pigott.

Scottish Mountaineering Club Journal—
Vol. I. *Three Days among the Cuchullins*, W. W. Naismith.
  Sgurr Alasdair, C. Pilkington.
Vol. II. *A Day in the Cuillins*, A. E. Maylard.
  Skye and Sgurr nan Gillean in 1865, Alex. Nicolson.
  On the Height of Some of the Black Cuchullins, J. N. Collie.
  Easter in the Cuillins, J. H. Gibson.
  The Pinnacle Route, W. W. Naismith.
  Sgurr Dearg Pinnacle, W. Brunskill.
Vol. III. *Bidein Druim nan Ramh*, W. Tough.
  Bhasteir and Bhasteir Tooth, F. W. Jackson.
Vol. IV. *Clach Glas, Skye*, F. W. Jackson.
  Sgurr, Dubh, Skye, W. Douglas.
  The Coolins in 1896, W. Brown.
  A Chuilionn, Norman Collie.

Vol. v. *The Climber's Camp at Coruisk*, W. Douglas.
August at Sligachan, G. Bennett Gibbs.
Early Descriptions of Skye, compiled by the Editor.
The Storr Rock, H. Raeburn.
Vol. vi. *Notes, Geological and Topographical, on the Cuillin Hills, Skye*, Alfred Harker.
Maccoitar's Cave Skye, Scott Moncrieff Penney.
Cloudless March Days in Skye, Scott Moncrieff Penney.
Stormy June Days in Skye, etc., W. Inglis Clark.
Vol. vii. *Sligachan to Glenbrittle by the Dubh Ridges*, W. N. Ling.
Beallach Coire Labain, J. A. Parker.
A Spring Day on Blaven, C. Walker.
Sligachan Meet Easter 1903.
Vol. viii. *Only a Beautiful Day on the Hills*, A. E. Maylard.
Silgachan Meet, Easter 1905.
Vol. ix. *Ridge-walking on the Coolins at Easter 1905*, H. Raeburn.
The Castles from Harta Corrie, H. Raeburn.
Hot Nights and Days on the Mountains in June, H. T. Munro.
Glen Brittle in June, H. MacRobert.
Bhasteir Tooth, L. G. Shadbolt.
The Island of Skye, (Guide Book), W. Douglas
Vol. x. *A Skye Highway*, Will. C. Smith.
Letter from G. Bennett Gibbs, *A Trip to Sligachan and Glen Brittle.*
The Cuillins in a Week, J. A. Parker.
Midsummer Days in Skye, Francis Greig.
Vol. xi. *Sligachan Meet, Easter 1911.*
The Cuillin Main Ridge, L. G. Shadbolt.
Sgurr Alasdair, Francis Greig.
Vol. xii. *New Climbs in Skye*, J. M. Archer Thomson.
The Unseen Corrie and The Dubhs, J. R. Young.
Wanderings on the Cuillin, Jas. C. Thomson.
Bidein Druim nan Ramh, W. W. Naismith.
Vol. xiii. *The Gullies of Coire an Uaigneis*, E. W. Steeple.
Some Walks in Skye, Wm. Galbraith.
Eastern Faces of Blaven and Clach Glas, Jas. C. Thomson.
Vol. xiv. *On Some Old Maps*, A. Harker.
Sassenachs in Skye, J. Hirst.
Nomenclature of the Cuillin, Colin B. Phillip.
Some Memories of Skye, J. H. Buchanan.

1

Sleat

(1)	**Sgurr na Coinnich**	2401 ft.
(2)	**Beinn na Caillich**	2306 ft.
(3)	**Beinn Aslak**	1984 ft.

One does not go to Sleat to climb mountains. This long south-eastern peninsula of Skye is as full of charm, as it is of boggy moor and delectable lochans. In the south its numerous eminences are featureless, and its chief joy lies along its coast. There are many fine situations. Of note particularly are Tarskavaig and the point of Sleat. The former can be reached by a narrow and winding road, the latter by a two-mile walk beyond the road end at Aird of Sleat.

Only in the north does the region heave itself into mountainous form. A knot of forbidding hills runs steeply down into the inner sea loch of Loch Alsh. Perhaps more than any other feature, they impart to the visitor arriving from the east the sense of the end of the world, a curtain beyond which it seems that no further habitation could exist.

Sgurr na Coinnich (2401 ft.)

This scree-topped peak, together with its neighbour to the north, Beinn na Caillich presents a forbidding wall of green to the visitor poised on the slipway at the Glenelg side of the Caolas Rhea (Kylerhea) Car Ferry. From the Skye side (poor camping) at Kylerhea a steep and most attractive road rises up Kylerhea glen. It is best to keep to the road till the Bealach Udal (900 ft.) (parking on east side) from which the south shoulder may be easily gained. This gives the driest and pleasantest ascent. There are rocks to tempt the scrambler. A traverse including Beinn na Caillich may be rounded off by a descent to the Loch Alsh shore, for there is a convenient path along Kylerhea, back to the ferry slipway at Kylerhea.

3. Sgurr nan Gillean and the Bhasteir group from the north.

4. East coast of Skye – the view out from near Loch Ainort with Beinn na Caillich in the distant centre.

Beinn na Caillich (2396 ft.)

This is the peak immediately obvious on the Skye shore when waiting at Kyles (Coalas) Lochalsh looking above the ruins of Caisteal Maol. It is, as stated above, best approached from Sgurr na Coinnich by the north east ridge. Having gained the top, which is a fine view point, one could, if intent on a traverse, continue N.N.W. along a ridge of grass and rock slabs towards the head of Loch na Beiste, and gain Kyleakin over the low col N.N.E. of the loch-head. Fig. 5.

Beinn Aslak (1984 ft.)

This peak is almost doomed to oblivion, since it is part of the three square miles of Skye that does not appear on the O.S. (7th series) one-inch maps of Skye. In fact it appears in the N.W. corner of Sheet 35 (Loch Arkaig). It is a rather fine little peak, easily ascended by the N.W. ridge from the Bealach Udal on the Kylerhea–Breakish road, and because of the miles of intervening bog, unlikely to be ascended from any other point. It offers an excellent viewpoint southwards down the Sound of Sleat and into the finest of all sea lochs, Loch Hourn. There are some decaying buttresses on the north flank facing Kylerhea glen.

2

Strathaird

(1)	Beinn na Caillich	2403 ft.
(2)	Beinn Dearg Mor	2323 ft.
(3)	Glas Bheinn Mor	1852 ft.
(4)	Belig	2250 ft.
(5)	Garbh Bheinn	2649 ft.
(6)	Sgurr nan Each	2360 ft.
(7)	Clach Glas	2590 ft.
(8)	Blaven (Bla Bheinn)	3042 ft.
(9)	Sgurr Hain	1200 ft.
(10)	Beinn na Cros	1750 ft. approx.

Strathaird comprises some of the most picturesque, some of the grandest and some of the doucest scenery in Skye. For the purposes of this guide it will be taken as that ground west of the Broadford–Elgol road but east of the Cuillin on a line drawn from Harta Corrie in the Cuillin to Loch Ainort on the east coast.

The 13 miles from Broadford (hotels, post office, shops, garages) to Elgol (shop, post office), is one of the finest journeys to be made. Yet no real hint of this is suggested in the first few miles along Strath Suardal. To one's right are the scree massifs of Beinn na Caillich, to the left bleak moorland.

As the road turns west there is the first stupendous glimpse of the Blaven massif, and the eye is carried down Loch Slapin to the island of Rhum. Elgol lies at the end of the peninsula on the west side of loch Slapin, and reserves its surprises to the last moment.

There are two important walking routes. There is a four-mile path through the narrow glen of Strathmor from the head of Loch Slapin to Luib on Loch Ainort. The path shown on the east side is a deception and one finds much better going on the west. It is not an attractive route. More interesting is the glen to east, Strathbeag (5 miles) which cuts through to Strollamus opposite Scalpay.

In the Elgol peninsula there is the important access route from Kirkibost [Kilmarie] to Camusunary ($1\frac{1}{2}$ hours). This path, once excellent, is currently (1969) in a woeful state due to attempts to widen it to a car track (see Coir' Uisg). Camusunary itself is one of the finest coastal sites in Scotland. The shooting lodge there is uninhabited, and was once a farm. It was brought to life in Mary Stewart's novel: Wild Fire at Midnight. Half a mile further west along the shore is a dilapidated lodge. The path continues round the base of Sgurr na Stri to Scavaig. There is now a useful suspension bridge over the Abhain Camus Fhionaridh (original spelling of this place: same pronunciation).

It is also possible to reach Camusunary from Elgol (2 hours), though the first stretch from the village on a high line along the steep grass slopes under Carn Mor is wearisome. Later there is a path which gets better as one approaches Camusunary. Though a longer route than from Kirkibost, the scene before one is so magnificent that the weight of one's rucksack is a trifle.

Scavaig may be reached by boat from Elgol or Mallaig, and there are usually fishermen willing to charter their boats for the journey.

The east side of the peninsula, called Glasnakille, contains a number of delightfully situated crofts. Below the telephone kiosk is the Spar cave, 300 yards deep, with a small lochan in it.*

Beinn Cleat (800 ft.) is accessible from just behind the Elgol Post Office, and though it has crags (Carn Mor) on the west side, they offer no climbing. Ben Meabost (1128 ft.) has a line of crags along its east rim, visible from the road. The hill is best reached from the road before Elgol.

Beinn na Caillich (2403 ft. Peak of the Old Woman)

One should not dismiss this unprepossessing mountain. It is one of a group comprising Beinn Dearg Mor (2323 ft. Great Red Peak) and Beinn Dearg Bheag (1900 ft. Little Red Peak) and Beinn na Caillich. They are formed of red granite which has weathered into a rounded form, and though vestigial crags remain, they have no attraction for the climber. As view points they are superb. Beinn na Caillich is best ascended from Coire-chat-achan, gained either by walking from the high point (140 ft.) of Suardal two miles south of Broadford, or following the track that runs south from the A850, a mile west of Broadford. This route also provides the least onerous ascent of the other summits, by entering Coire Beithe.

* See section on 'Geology'.

Glas-Bheinn Mor (1852 ft. The Great Grey Peak)

Is the northern outrider of the Blaven group, but unlike them not composed of gabbro. Its sharp spine shows well from the Broadford–Sligachan road at Luib, from which it may be easily ascended. It is rarely climbed for itself, but taken as a round with Gars-Bheinn it makes an enjoyable hill walk.

Beinn na Cros (1750 ft. approx)

The southern aspect of this peak is of a steep and dreary scree. It is a steep little hill, and may only be ascended with ease from the north.

BLACK CUILLIN OUTRIDERS

Belig (2250 ft. approx)

This is a shapely little peak. The col between Glas Bheinn Mor and Belig lies at 1300 ft. From the south the peak may be climbed direct up its S.S.E. ridge from the head of Loch Slapin or most pleasantly from the col with Glas-Bheinn Mor. It has small crags, but its climbing potential is untested. Photo 7.

Garbh-Bheinn (2649 ft. The Rough Mountain)

For all its name, which is apt, there are few crags to tempt the climber. Those on the N.E. face have the greatest potential. The ridge linking Belig is the finest (col 1300 ft.). It also throws down ridges towards Clach Glas (south) and north towards the head of Loch Ainort. From the south it would normally be ascended via the intervening summit of Sgurr nan Each. On the N.W. ridge at 1500 ft. is a 300 ft. buttress with no recorded routes.

Sgurr nan Each (West top, 2360 ft. Peak of the Horses)

This top lies ¾ mile east of Garbh-Bheinn and 1 mile N.E. of Blaven. It is readily ascended by its S.E. ridge from the Allt na Dunaiche, near the head of Loch Slapin. The col between it and Clach Glas is 2050 ft. Below this col are some broken buttresses offering some 400 ft. of difficult climbing and agreeable access to the ridge. Photo 7.

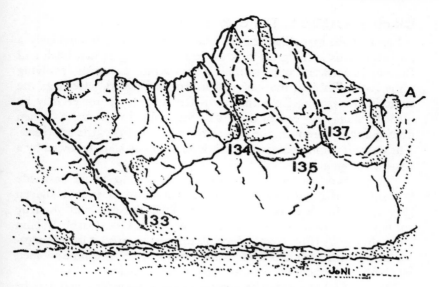

Fig. 1. Clach Glas – West face

A	Blaven-Clach Glas bealach	133	Arch Gully
B	Black Cleft (unclimbed)	134	Consolation Gully
		135	Naismith's Route
		137	Pilkington's Route

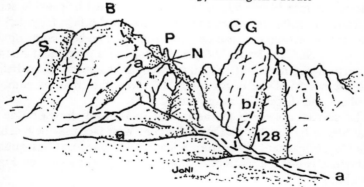

Fig. 2. Blaven and Clach Glas from East

B	Blaven	a–a	easiest route to Blaven
CG	Clach Glas	b–b	easiest route to Clach Glas
N	Northwall, East ridge	128	A-gully
P	Naismith's 'half-crown' Pinnacle		
S	South buttress		

Clach Glas (2590 ft. The Grey Stone)

Earlier O.S. maps had this as Clac Glas, but this is obviously a misprint. This is the great rock tower between Sgurr nan Each and Blaven. The traverse of its summit is a rewarding excursion involving some rock climbing, most of which can be avoided, save near the summit. Traversing from the north the final 30 ft. tower may be turned taking the conspicuous slanting gully to the west. When descending to the south, the easiest ground is always to the left (east). The descent commences with a crack on a sloping slab, followed by a narrow rotten arête.

The col between Clach Glas and Garbh Bheinn on the east side is a simple, if rough, walk, as is the col between it and Blaven [Fig 2]. At the latter there is a tower – Bealach tower, and the true col lies to its south. On the west side of Clach Glas-Garbh Bheinn col is *Arch gully* [Fig. 1, 33] which, if adhered to, gives a long moderate climb with a big chock stone pitch half way up. It can be avoided by climbing initially up scree towards Garbh Bheinn.

The east face is of steep broken rock with grass ledges, and may be traversed in many places. The principal feature is two gullies that start from the lowest rocks and finish on the north ridge. The left hand is V.D. [128, Fig. 2], the right hand gives 8 hard pitches from the lowest rocks and finishes on the north ridge. To the climber the angle of the face is not steep, but under snow it can provide some interesting ascents. An ascending rake crosses the face from left to right, and affords an easy ascent. [b-b Fig. 2]. The best route on the east side is *Sickle* (280 ft. V.S.) which follows a prominent line on the vertical north wall of the first tower (as it appears from below from the north) of the north ridge. The west face may be climbed anywhere and difficulties never exceed V.D.

The eastern approach to the mountain is from the east side of Loch Slapin by the Allt na Dunaiche. The west face may be reached from Glen Sligachan, either from Sligachan (4 hours) or Camusunary (1½ hours). It offers a number of climbs of no great merit: see Fig 1 and photo 8.

Blaven or Bla Bheinn (3042 ft. Hill of Bloom)

The superb mountain, isolated and beautifully located, terminates the ridge that has been described. Southwards is only sea. Sheriff Nicolson considered it the finest hill in Skye, and Alexander Smith wrote:

"At a clear open turn in the roadway
My passion went up with a cry,
For the wonderful mountain of Blaven
Was heaving his huge bulk on high"

The traverse of the peak [see Fig. 2], coupled with Clach Glas is a classic expedition. However, from the Bealach, route finding can be difficult in mist due to the number of apparent possibilities. Traversing from north to south, steep rocks are avoided on the left by an easy 12 ft. wall. Cross some scree to the right, pass one chimney and ascend the next, which is a stone shoot. It leads to a scree platform at the upper (eastern) end of which stands Naismith's ("Half Crown") pinnacle. Traverse this scree platform to the left for a few yards, then climb a 60 ft. chimney. At its head cross some big stones, and descend to enter a large stone shoot, which may be ascended to the sky-line, and hence to the summit. Sportier routes, of course, may be taken.

The stone shoot just referred to can be used to descend the mountain. It leads right into Coire Dubh on the west side, well below the Clach Glas Blaven bealach.

By contrast the south ridge of the mountain may be ascended from Camusunary without difficulty.

Close under the S. top of Blaven stands South Buttress, which has recently yielded some fine climbs. The most prominent feature is a sweeping pillar of pale slabs to the left, *Central Pillar* (650 ft. Severe). The gully to its left is still unclimbed. Left again is *Belinda*, a shorter route on a smaller buttress, while right of the *Centre Pillar* are several routes from Difficult to Severe till near the right hand edge of the buttress is the fine route: *The Hem* (600 ft. Severe). For several of these climbs pitons are needed as belays.

The east face is somewhat like Clach Glas with long easy routes, but it harbours a North Wall, [N, Fig 2 and Photo 8] one section of which rises 400 ft. It is bounded on the right by a magnificent rib, above and behind which lies an easy gully, which is a useful means of ascent. The wall continues and ultimately connects with the north ridge near the Half Crown Pinnacle (see above). The routes here are all hard and provide some excellent climbing. *Sidewinder*, *Great Prow* and *Main Wall* are on the main wall. *The Horn* ascends the east face of the Half Crown pinnacle. Approaching from the east the peak is gained by Coire Uaigneich (easiest route), or by one of the Clach Glas cols. The western approach must be rare. The energetic walker coming from Sligachan should follow the path till Loch an Athain, and then either follow the stone shoot directly to the skyline ridge of the north top, which is purgatorial if technically easy, or more advisedly make for one of the Clach Glas cols. Blaven's western flanks are disappointing. The Pinnacle ridge, seen in profile from Loch an Athain, offers a short easy climb after a long scree haul.

Sgurr Hain

This name applies to the massif above and to the west of Lochan na Creithach just above Camusunary, and to the east of Lochan Coire Riabhach. It has gabbro cliffs of 300 ft. facing S.E. upon which no climbs have yet been reported.

5. Beinn na Caillich from Glen Elg.

6. The Black Cuillin from Elgol.

7. Crofting beneath the Cuillins, at Kilbride. Left to right: Blaven, Clach Glas, Sgurr nan Each, Garbh-bheinn, Belig.

8. Blaven and Clach Glas, across Loch Slapin.

3

The Red Cuillin

(1)	Glamaig	2537 ft.
(2)	Beinn Dearg Mhor	2389 ft.
(3)	Marsco	2414 ft.
(4)	Ruadh Stac	1750 ft.

These hills are well named. They are red, being composed of red granite. They are almost free from sheets and dykes so that the smooth flowing outline of the peaks here are determined by the crumbling of the granite, almost uninterrupted by intrusions. When dykes occur, they tend to project above the surface and not form gullies as in the Black Cuillin.

These hills have a wretched reputation, to a great extent unjustified. For though their flanks are almost everywhere reduced to scree, the peaks have a fine distinctive shape, each is isolated, and they offer the hill-walker some wonderful vistas.

Though physically connected to the Black Cuillin of the Blaven group, they are in every other way different. The boundary is clearly visible either to the walker on the ground or to the observer from the main ridge. On the Garbh-Bheinn side of the Marsco-Garbh Bheinn col the red suddenly changes into black. The acute and craggy nature of Garbh Bheinn stands out in comparison to the flowing lines of Marsco.

The group is bounded on the west by Glen Sligachan, and on the east by Loch Ainort. It presents one simple ridge from Glamaig in the north to Marsco 4 miles to the south, with an outrider called Ruadh Stac above Loch na Creithach. The new road from the head of Loch Ainort to Sconser climbs over the shoulder of Druim na Gleochd, and runs down the Glen Torra Mhichaig, bringing the eastern flanks within easy reach of the motorist. The top of this road is some 430 ft. and lies less than a mile from the summit of Beinn Dearg Mhor (2389 ft).

As a complete and satisfying ridge walk one may start from the 1079 ft. col S.E. of Marsco and finish at Glamaig.

Glamaig (2537 ft.)

The highest top is named Sgurr Mhairi, after a girl killed while seeking a cow. The east summit is called An Coileach.

From Sligachan it appears as a rounded cone, though in fact there is a summit ridge of some ¾ of a mile. It is steep on all sides, and no best route can be recommended. Tradition has it that one of the pioneers ascended it in 37 minutes from Sligachan, and descended in 18 minutes. Two hours is the more likely time to the average walker. It is readily accessible from Sconser, and the least painful ascent is by the Bealach na Sgairde (1419 ft.) to the north by either of the burns to east or west.

Beinn Dearg Mhor (2389 ft. The Big Red Peak)

This peak has a long summit ridge of almost 2½ miles. It comprises three tops divided by the Bealach Mosgaraidh (1663 ft.). On the east side the burn running from this col passes close to the Ainort-Sconser road at about the 300 foot contour. This is a good starting point. The north end, north of the bealach is the highest point, and south of the bealach is Beinn Dearg Mheadhonach (Middle Red Peak) and the end point, Ciche na Beinne Dearge (The Pap of the Red Hill). South of this the hill falls to a col at 952 ft., called the Mam a'Phobuill. To the walker wishing to traverse the peak, this is the obvious route of approach. The road at Loch Ainort head is 2 miles off, via Coire na Bruadron, while Sligachan is some 3 miles distant via Coire Dubh Measarroch.

Marsco (2414 ft.)

This peak is a fine viewpoint. It sprouts a buttress on its west side, clearly visible in side lighting from the Black Cuillin and seen in profile from Glen Sligachan. It faces Sgurr na-h-Uamha. The rock, a coarse dusty granophyre, gives climbing of a completely different character to gabbro. Three routes are recorded (1969). *Odell's* (600 ft. D.) rises from the central amphitheatre, and makes for the shoulder above the prominent central buttress. Wrangham's *Central Buttress* (550 ft. V.D.) starts at the foot of the buttress and chooses a direct line. *Boojum* V.S., lies on the Sligachan Face.

The bealach between Marsco and Garbh-Bheinn (1079 ft.) is just as accessible as Mam a'Phobuill from the head of Loch Ainort, but the south side takes a good half hour longer to reach from Sligachan.

Ruadh Stac (1750 ft. approx. The Red Stack)

Craggy and scree ridden, it is interesting by virtue of its separation from the higher hills to either side.

4

Minginish and the Cuillin

(1)	**Black Cuillin**	(see page 80)
(2)	**An Huaranan**	800 ft. approx.
(3)	**Preshal Mor**	950 ft.
(4)	**Preshal Beag**	1100 ft.

The Cuillin are in Minginish, but Minginish is not the Cuillin. This highly varied terrain lies in the sector to the south and west of Sligachan. Of course, the black fins and glistening slabs of these, perhaps the finest peaks in the British Isles, dominate the landscape. There are three centres for the Cuillin, which are noted below. Before embarking on the guide book description of these mountains, the rest of the area will be treated.

CORUISK: See later section 1: Coir' Uisg.

SLIGACHAN

The newcomer to Minginish is almost certain to arrive via Sligachan. Here, a mile inland from the top of Loch Sligachan and close by the junction of the Allt Dearg and the Sligachan River, stands one of Skye's most famous hostelries, Sligachan Inn. [Photo 9]. Known equally by fishers and climbers, this fine old inn was the home from home for the early breed of Victorian explorers. Here the great names of the Alpine Club and the Scottish Mountaineering Club used to foregather. Their exploits were recorded in the Sligachan book. And with island malt whiskies, the wet evenings and terrible drenchings of south-westerlies were forgotten, and tales were told of bold climbs and virgin peaks. The Inn still welcomes climbers, though a notice requests them not to climb upon the lounge walls.

There is no convenient free camping at Sligachan. A bleak field is made available nearby. The best to be had comes by carrying one's camp southward up Glen Sligachan into the Harta Coire. Thus most people are driven to Glen Brittle.

GLEN BRITTLE

One may walk to Glen Brittle from Sligachan (3 hours). The route is wearisome and the going boggy. It is recommended only to the impecunious and austere. From the Carbost road, 500 yards from Sligachan take the road to Allt Dearg House, and follow the path, initially good, up the burn of the same name. It crosses the Bealach a Mhaim and lands one at the top of the Glen, from whence the metalled road is gained.

The road from Sligachan follows the incredibly dreary Glen Drynoch to the head of Loch Harport, where a turning is taken from Carbost. This small crofting township is famous for its distillery, Talisker, which makes one of the finest malt whiskies to be bought. The colour of a Cuillin burn in spate, this whisky has a rich aromatic flavour. It is not normally sold under 8 years of age, and another couple of years works wonders.

From Carbost the climber and walker will normally head over the moor road to Glen Brittle. It is not a strikingly beautiful glen. A forestry plantation on the west side has done a little to relieve the drabness of the hillsides, but when mist obliterates the Cuillin, the scene has little to recommend it. The Youth Hostel is situated two miles from the sea at the bridge over the Allt a' Choire Ghreadaidh. It is a cheerless location, but stategic for the mountains. A mile down the road is the B.M.C. memorial hut, and beyond that the few houses of the Glen. The principal house, Glenbrittle House, has long offered accommodation to climbers, and it has historical associations with the early days of exploration. At the mouth of the river on the west side at Bualintur several houses offer accommodation. By keeping to the east of the river past Glen Brittle house, one comes on the greensward by the beach, now Scotland's most densely occupied camping ground. Here is a shop, climbing school and toilets. It is the only camping permitted in the glen, unless one carries a camp into the corries.

The Cuillin are described in detail, at the end of this section, and will not be considered here. For the walker tied by weather or inclination to the lower ground, the environs of Glen Brittle offer little. The shore is of black rock, and occasionally black sand, The cliff scenery is not the best Skye has to offer. A path of sorts works along the cliff tops on the east shore of Loch Brittle towards the point, Rubha' an Dunain. As the name implies, there is here an old Dun to which the path leads. About a mile from the point the path turns due south, and here a defile runs deeply across the narrow peninsula, appropriately called in Gaelic, the Black Drain, or Slochd Dubh. The south shore of this peninsula is much more interesting. The land behind rises more steeply, and dozens of fascinating little coves are to be found. Just across the Sound of Soay is the Island of the same name. See p. 163.

In Glen Brittle in summer tourist boats will occasionally enter the Loch and offer trips to Rhum or round to Loch Scavaig. Most climbers will couple this with a crossing of the Cuillin main ridge by one or other of the routes, but some will walk back along the coast. Though at the Scavaig end there is a path under the steep eastern flank of Gars-bheinn, this path peters out as it turns the south flank of the mountain. The walk over the moor back to Glen Brittle is long and tiring, though on a good day, well worth it.

The coast line on the north shore of Loch Brittle is steep and difficult to traverse. By keeping to the 500 foot contour one is led to An Crocan beyond which the coastal scenery is magnificent. This side offers fine views of the Cuillin. A mile inland the moorland summit of Beinn an Eoin (1023 ft.) offers superb vistas east and west.

A path leads N.W. out of the Glen to neighbouring Glen Eynort. A forestry road leads behind the B.M.C. hut, crosses the river Brittle, and as a path leads up through the plantation, crossing the Bealach Brittle at about 780 feet. After a short time it meets a forestry road coming up from the other side.

EYNORT AND FISKAVAIG:

The path described above descends through a plantation on the east side of Loch Eynort. The glen, steep and narrow with little cultivatable land is reached by a narrow road from Carbost. The community is largely given over to forestry.

The coast line from Eynort round to Fiskavaig in the north end of Minginish is magnificent. In places the cliffs are 900 feet high. Save for Talisker Bay, the coast is unpopulated. Inland is a region of indeterminate hills and lochs of which three, An Huaranan, Preshal Beag (1100 ft.) and Preshal Mor (950 ft.) have cliffs which offer climbing. They are most easily reached by driving from Carbost on the Gleann Orraid road. This glen opens out into Talisker bay, black-sanded with black cliffs, (Sron Mhor), and one basaltic stack.

Preshal Mor presents a ragged face to the north, with a deep gully. To the south it presents a significant wall of cliffs of about 300 ft.

An Huaranan is a long escarpment on Arnaval (1210 ft.), 300 ft. above and to the north of the Gleann Orraid road.

Fiskavaig is gained by a road north from Carbost and is a rambling crofting township in a superb situation. A path leads through to Gleann Orraid.

The Cuillin

The Cuillin Hills. Taken in order from the most southerly northwards.

(1) **Gars-Bheinn,** 2935 ft. (Sections 2, 13) Pron. garsven = echoing mountain. N.G 468187.
(2) **Sgurr a' Choire Bhig,** 2872 ft. (2, 13) Pron. Sgur a corrie vik = peak of the little corrie.
(3) **Sgurr nan Eag,** 3031 ft. (2, 12, 13) = notched peak.
(4) **Caisteal a Garbh Choire,** 2719 ft. (2) = castle of the rough corrie.
(5) **Sgurr Dubh Mor,** 3096 ft. (2, 3) = the big black peak.
(6) **Sgurr Dubh na Da Bheinn,** 3078 ft. (3, 12) = the black peak of the two hills.
(7) **Sgurr Sgumain,** 3108 ft. (11, 12) = the stack peak.
(8) **Sgurr Alaisdair,** 3257 ft. (11) = Alexander's peak.
(9) **Sgurr Thearlaich,** 3208 ft. (3, 11, 12) = Charlie's peak.
(10) **Sgurr Mhic Coinnich,** 3111 ft. (4, 11) = McKenzie's peak.
(11) **An Stac,** 3125 ft. (4, 11) = the stack.
(12) **Sgurr Dearg,** 3209 ft. (4, 10, 11) = the red peak.
(13) **Sgurr na Banachdich,** 3166 ft. (4, 10) = smallpox peak.
(14) **Sgurr Thormaid,** 3040 ft. (4, 9) = Norman's peak.
(15) **Sgurr a' Ghreadaidh,** 3192 ft. (4, 5) = peak of the thrashings.
(16) **Sgurr a' Mhadaidh,** 3012 ft. (5, 8) Pron. Sgur a vatee = foxes peak.
(17) **Bidein Druim nan Ramh,** 2850 ft. (5, 6, 8) Pron. Bidyin drim nan rav = peak of the ridge of oars.
(18) **Bruach na Frithe,** 3143 ft. (6, 7, 8) Pron. Bruach na free = brae of the forest.
(19) **Am Bhasteir,** 3069 ft. (6, 7) Pron. Am Vasteer = the executioner.
(20) **Sgurr nan Gillean,** 3167, ft. (6, 7) = the peak of the young men. NG. 475253.

The Cuillin hills are one single ridge approximately 7 miles long with outriders. Therein are contained 11 Munros. The narrowness of the crests, the steepness of the mountain faces, and the sculpturing of the corries has resulted in a mountain group of great character. From Gars Bheinn in the S.W. of Minginish, above the shore of Loch Scavaig the chain of peaks runs north west, turns N.N.E. at Sgurr na Banachdich as far as Sgurr a' Mhadaidh, passes through its lowest point at the head of the Coir' Uisg and bends north at the Bruach na Frithe, the easiest summit of the range. It then turns sharply east to a final triumphant upsurge at Sgurr nan Gillean. For three-quarters of the distance, the mountains press in on Loch Coruisk, whose waters are visible only from some peaks. Beyond Sgurr a' Mhadaidh, one looks east to the less imposing Harta corrie. Mean-

9. Sligachan Inn.

10. The Black Cuillin in winter from north of Carbost. The large
snowfilled corrie in the centre is Coire na Creiche. To its left is
Bruach na Frithe. The leftmost peak is Sgurr nan Gillean, the
rightmost is Sgurr Dearg, under which lies Glen Brittle.

while to westward magnificent corries swoop down to boggy moorlands at about 1200 ft. Fortunately as one toils upwards one has the
stimulating prospect of the mountains ahead, while on the descent,
the ever changing sea scapes release the mind from the dullness
underfoot.

To describe each mountain in a chain so closely linked would be
merely confusing. The system adopted is to give a description of
each corrie under a numbered section. Since most peaks occur in
at least two corries, full details can only be had by consulting both
sections. In the list heading this chapter the relevant alternative
corries are indicated after each peak. Within each section will be
given some of the salient rock climbing routes and a broad description thereof. The routes numbers are those used in the SMT rock
guide. For detailed instructions the reader should consult the two
S.M.C. rock climbing guides to the area.

In addition to the above method of description, in section 16 the
information is presented as if the reader was moving along the ridge
itself. Section 14 considers the Cuillin traverse and section 15 winter
climbing.

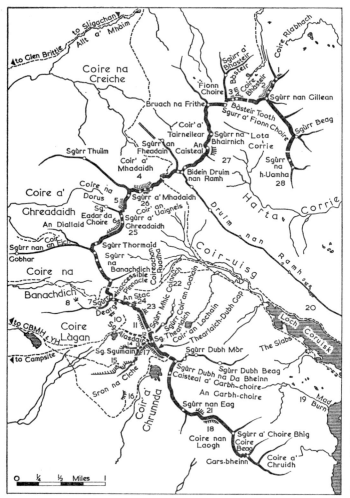

1 1st Pinnacle, Sligacha
   Face
2 Pinnacle Ridge and ...
   nan Gillean
3 Am Bhasteir and Bha
   Tooth
4 Sgurr a'Mhadaidh, N
   Face
5 Sgurr a'Ghreadaidh,
   N.W. Face
6 Sgurr a'Ghreadaidh, ...
   Face
7 Sgurr Dearg, NW Bu
8 Sgurr Dearg, Windo...
   Buttress
9 Inaccessible Pinnacle
10 Sgurr Dearg, S. But...
11 Sgurr Mhic Coinnich
   Buttress
12 Sgurr Thearlaich
13 Sgurr Alasdair
14 Sgurr Sgumain
15 Sron na Ciche
16 Sron na Ciche, S. C...
17 Sgurr Alasdair, Ghru...
   Face
18 Coire nan Laogh
19 Mad Burn Buttress
20 Coruisk Face, Bidein
   Druim nan Ramh
21 Sgurr nan Eag
   Caisteal a'Gharbh-ch
   Sgurr Dubh
22 Sgurr Coir'an Lochai
23 Sgurr Mhic Coinnich
24 Bealach Buttress
   Sgurr Dearg
   Sgurr na Banachdich
25 Sgurr a'Ghreadaidh
26 Coire an Uaigneis
27 An Caisteal
   Bhasteir Tooth
28 Sgurr na h'Uamha

COIR' UISG

---

(1)	**Sgurr na Stri**	1632 ft.
(2)	**Meall na Cuilce**	400 ft.
(3)	and **Coire Riabhach**	

Coir' Uisg is the heart of the Cuillin. Also written Coire Uisge, it has been anglicized to Coruisk, and is now generally but incorrectly spelt this way. It is an appropriate name, meaning corrie of water. The name does not apply to any high corrie, but the lower slopes of that cirque of high corries and jagged peaks that ring the top end of Loch Coruisk. The Loch is a sheet of water two miles long, lying among the glacier-polished slabs of lower Coir' Uisg. Its banks are a mixture of slabs and peat bogs, and may be negotiated easily, if soddenly, on either side. The S.W. side offers the best going.

300 yards of fast flowing river connect the S.W. end of the loch with the sea. Over the years a series of stepping stones have been built, adequate for a crossing save in high spate. In 1968 Army engineers erected a suspension bridge (which no climbers or walkers wanted: see S.M.C.J. 1969). It stands $6\frac{1}{2}$ feet above low water, and since Coruisk has been known (e.g. July 1949) to rise 8 ft. in one day, the durability of this bridge is in doubt*. In spate the burn is a danger, and if swept off one's feet, one would inevitably finish in the sea at Loch na Cuilce.

At the outlet of the river into the sea is a small island. North of this and west of the river mouth is a superb anchorage, with deep water right in-shore. Tourist boats from Mallaig can land alongside the iron steps provided.

Here are a number of campsites, using the flat, but moisture retaining, peat-grass terrain. Sewn-in ground sheets are useful.

The sea loch here is called Scavaig, and the inner portion Loch na Cuilce. The sail into Cuilce from Scavaig is one of the finest to be made in the British Isles. Photo 14. The impending mountain

* In October, 1969 both this bridge and that at Camusunary were destroyed by gales.

walls, and constantly changing serrated skyline are excitement in themselves, but the discovery of the desolate haven behind the islets and under the crags of Meall na Cuilce is excitement of another sort. In the N.E. corner under a vertical cliff stands the small square green roofed 'Coruisk Memorial Hut', open to all affiliated to the B.M.C. or A.S.S.C. or by special arrangement. It holds nine, has running water, coal and bottled gas. This point, though not actually at Loch Coruisk, is always referred to as 'Coruisk'.

The situation, though magnificent, is a trap. After prolonged heavy rain one may be unable to escape shorewards either toward Camusunary and Strathaird or to Glen Brittle.

There only are only three routes to civilization that do not involve a major river crossing:

(1) the ascent of An Garbh Choire (section 2 and photo 13) into upper Coire a' Ghrunnda, across it to the Bealach a' Ghrunnda (section 11) and down to Coire Lagan;

(2) the complex traverse of the Bealach Mhic Coinnich; or

(3) traverse of the Bealach Banachdich.

Access for those staying at Coruisk is usually by boat from Elgol (special arrangement) or Mallaig (occasional tourist boat), or by foot from Strathaird (which see). This route passes Camusunary and follows the south base of Sgurr na Stri ($1\frac{1}{2}$ hours from Camusunary, 3 hours from Kirkibost and Strathaird). At one point the steep crags of Sgurr na Stri fall right into the sea, and the walker is forced to use his hands. The route is obvious, a deep crack in the slab, and the handholds are generous. (See Sgurr na Stri). Photo 15.

The walking route to Glen Brittle is not devoid of technical difficulty. From the Coruisk hut head south on the west shore of Scavaig. Within 200 yards a rib or rock forces one into some delicate rock climbing, much harder than the so-called 'Bad Step' on the route to Camusunary. By following a crack upwards, an easier line is found. Thereafter the route crosses the Mad Burn (see An Garbh Choire section 2). The shore may be followed for the next 3 miles to the burn issuing from Coire an Laoigh. Follow this up to the 1000 ft. contour and then follow the N.W. contour to Glen Brittle ($2\frac{1}{2}$ hours, 4 hours in all). This route involves crossing a difficult step 1 mile south of the Mad Burn, and the best route is in fact to make a climbing traverse from the Mad Burn to about 1000 ft. onto the S.E. shoulder of Garsbhein, and hold this height to meet the previous route on the Allt Coire an Laoigh.

Sgurr na Stri (1623 ft.)

This little mountain is one of the most impressive looking in the Cuillin, for it is steep-sided, and rises directly out of the sea. Unhappily, its mountainous quality is sullied by its numerous scattered tops. Situated to the east of the outfall of Loch Coruisk, at Loch Scavaig it dominates the sea loch and provides a superb view-point. Its flanks provide rocks of all standards. The south and west faces are the steepest and call for climbing, while access from the north via Loch a' Choire Riabhach is a straightforward walk. The south face falls straight into the sea with one or two vertical sections, and though the general angle is not high, it is steep enough to prevent the walker between Camusunary and Coruisk, passing without doing a little moderate climbing. A short section of slab cut by a wide easy crack links two well trodden sections of path, and is one of the delights of penetrating this remote spot. Commonly referred to as the '*Bad Step*', it has recently been the subject of considerable agitation, such as surrounds the destruction of an ancient memorial. An army territorial unit announced in 1968 its intention of blasting a path across the '*Bad Step*'. The climbing world rose up in arms. It was revealed that the request came from the Inverness-shire police who wanted an easier route for evacuating live casualties (to date there has been one). No one thought to consult the mountain rescue authorities. The present state of affairs is that the route from Strathaird to Camusunary is to be improved, but the '*Bad Step*', almost a national heirloom, is to remain inviolate.

It would be a great pity if this remarkable remote spot were to become as accessible as any suburban parkland. Its very isolation is half its charm to the visitor. Moreover the walker who does not wish to climb rocks at all can easily leave Coruisk by the path into Coire Riabhach and then make for the col to the north of Druim Hain (1000 ft.) and descend to Camusunary. Photo 17.

Coire Riabhach

This remote lonely little corrie, scarcely 500 ft. above Loch Coruisk harbours a charming lochan. Rocks of 50 to 200 ft. abound on the flanks of Sgurr na Stri to the south and Druim nan Ramh to the west. In a setting such as Coruisk, routes on these short crags scarcely merit names and descriptions, but they do provide delightful off-day exercise.

Meall na Cuilce (400 ft.)

This eminence rises directly to the west of the Memorial Hut For all its vegetation it provides some very hard rock climbing.

AN GARBH COIRE

(1)	**Sgurr Dubh na da Bheinn**	3078 ft.
(2)	**Sgurr Dubh Mor**	3096 ft.
(3)	**Sgurr Dubh Beag**	2403 ft.
(4)	**Sgurr nan Eag**	3031 ft.
(5)	**Sgurr a Choire Bheag**	2872 ft.
(6)	**Garsbheinn**	2935 ft.

This is one of the most magnificent of the Cuillin corries. Its name, meaning 'the rough corrie', is entirely appropriate. Not only is the floor of the corrie above 1500 feet a mass of huge gabbro boulder, whose negotiation calls for nimbleness and fitness, but the whole north wall is flanked by the beetling crags of the Sgurr Dubhs.

The Corrie lies immediately west of Loch Coruisk on the east side of the main ridge, and is a natural field of activity for those dwelling at Coruisk. Access to the corrie is guarded by the small bastion of Meall na Cuilce, N.W. of the hut. The easiest walking is to go to where the Scavaig river issues, and follow its right bank till one comes on Loch Coruisk. Easy walking over gentle gabbro slabs interspersed with Cuillin peat hags brings one in about twenty minutes to the corrie mouth. A small burn trickles down, and there can hardly be said to be any best route. There are numerous erratic boulders, slabs and tussocky grass. At about 700 ft. one crosses a small ridge into the corrie which flattens out a little. The main burn out of the corrie leaves this hollow and tumbles straight into Loch Scavaig (Allt a Chaoich).

Though the prospect up Loch Coruisk on the route just mentioned is something no visitor to Skye should miss, a considerably more interesting route to the bed of the corrie is to follow the side of the Allt a Chaoich, known also as the Mad Burn, that tumbles tempestuously down to inner Loch Scavaig (or more correctly, Loch na Cuilce) on the S.W. side of Meall na Cuilce. To gain this burn from the hut follow the shore. There is one very awkward rock step. It is no place for the pure walker. After a spate this burn can be impossible to cross (hence 'Mad' burn), a fact to bear in mind if making one's way down to the hut from the corrie. Nor can one avoid this difficulty by keeping to the N.E. side of the burn, because occasionally this demands a high level of rock climbing. On descent do not follow this burn but hold 100 yards to the S.W. on steep grass slopes. Having gained the bed of the corrie at 700 ft., all the peaks are accessible (see photo 13).

Garsbheinn (2935 ft. The Echoing Mountain), see also Coire on Laoigh [13]

This mountain, though not a Munro, is regarded as the true south end of the Cuillin main ridge. Its west and southern aspects are no more than unrelenting scree, and its summit ridge scarcely maintains the airy quality of the rest of the Cuillin. Nevertheless, as a view-point it is magnificent, with, of course, unobstructed view to Rhum and Canna, and a seemingly vertical view down to the blue ocean. The ascent from An Garbh Choire is the only one of real interest, with the N.E. ridge offering some mild scrambling near the top. The peak should not be treated casually in mist. It is girt with various small precipices on the Scavaig side, but its monotonous scree defences have so far dissuaded ciimbers from putting up new routes, though they undoubtedly exist.

Immediately under the peak on the north side lies an upper corrie, Coire Beag (marked O.S. map). The easiest descent on the Coruisk side is to follow the ridge towards Sgurr a' Coire Bhig, the next excrescence on the ridge northwards, till at a col at 2740 ft. one may drop into Coire Beag holding close under Sgurr a' Choire Bhig. Some rock climbing may be needed. Then bear well right to avoid the slabs. A stream out of the corrie leads one directly down to the floor of the main corrie. On the lower slopes are several small buttresses facing east. The lowest, *Mad Burn Buttress*, offers some excellent V.D.–S. routes.

Sgurr a' Choire Bhig (2872 ft. Peak of the Little Corrie), see also Coire on Laoigh [13]

This is a very pleasing little mountain, one mile north of Garsbheinn. The N.E. ridge is steep enough to be interesting and offers some slab climbing. On the north side is a small but fine crag. The two prominent gullies were climbed in 1921 by the legendary Steeple with Barlow and Doughty.

Sgurr nan Eag (3031 ft. Notched Peak), see also Coire a' Ghrunnda [12]

This Munro has a nearly level summit ridge lying S.E./N.W. for some 300 yards. The southern end has a spur or buttress, cleaved on the Coruisk side by an enormous cleft also climbed by Steeple and his friends. Below the ridge is a line of cliffs some 200 yards in extent up to 300 ft. high, offering some hard and interesting routes (e.g. *Ladders*, 360 ft. V.S.).

These difficulties are easily avoided, and the ascent of the peak from the corrie is rough going, but straightforward. It is natural to go for one or others of the cols. That to the south, 2537 ft. is the lowest.

Caisteal a Garbh Choire (2719 ft. Castle of the Rough Corrie), see also Coire a' Ghrunnda [12]

Between Sgurr nan Eag and this peak is an easy pass to Coire a' Ghrunnda at 2614 ft. This is not a peak but a craggy pimple of superbly rough gabbro on the Bealach which is a delight to play upon. The north end of the summit overhangs.

Sgurr Dubh na da Bheinn (3078 ft. Black Peak of the Two Tops), see also Coire a' Ghrunnda [12]

Though on the main ridge, this peak is outshone by its neighbours, being the western most of three Sgurr Dubhs. It is ascended without difficulty from this corrie, and is seldom an objective in itself. Its south and north flanks are steep and craggy.

Sgurr Dubh Mor (3096 ft. Great Black Peak)

This is a fine acutely-topped peak easily gained from the main ridge. Though it may be climbed easily from Sgurr Dubh na da Bheinn, or by meandering rock climbing up its south flank from the corrie, the usual approach is from Sgurr Dubh Beag in the course of one of the best excursions one can make in Skye. Its eastern flanks are little known. The S.E. ridge is not easy, while under the summit is a huge inaccessible slab, yet to be climbed.

Sgurr Dubh Beag (2403 ft. Little Black Peak)

One must put hand to rock to gain this summit. And though the Cuillin may offer more tempting summits, it offers none with a finer approach. For 2300 ft. one is rock climbing, albeit at a modest standard, for on the east side Sgurr Dubh Beag throws down a long 30° angled ridge of pure rock. From Coruisk the prospect is delightful indeed. A broad sweep of black dry slabs rise in endless overlaps. They are nowhere excessively steep, and though to fall off might in places be fatal, their roughness, their good quality, and their easy angle makes the eventuality unlikely. The following verses culled from an early S.M.C. journal give an excellent perspective to the east ridge:

'Said Maylard to Solly one day in Glen Brittle,
    All serious climbing, I vote, is a bore;
Just for once, I Dubh Beag you'll agree to do little,
    And, as less we can't do, let's go straight to Dubh Mor.

'So now when they seek but a day's relaxation,
    With no thought in the world but of viewing the views,
And regarding the mountains in mute adoration,
    They call it not "climbing," but "doing the Dubhs." '

The north and south flanks of Sgurr Dubh Beag are steep, and though there are pitches of great difficulty, the sloping terraces rob the faces of their character.

There is no water on the Dubh ridge. To gain Sgurr Dubh Mor from the Beag requires the descent of 50 very awkward feet of rock which overhang. A rope and the knowledge of how to use it are essential. Parties usually rappel this section, and it is no place to make one's first excursion into the art of roping down.

A common and delightful expedition is to leave from Loch Coruisk and ascend the east ridge (3 hours), traverse the other Sgurr Dubhs, from whence one may drop to Coire a' Ghrunnda and Glen Brittle, or traverse onwards to Sgurr Alaisdair, dropping by the Alaisdair stone shoot to Coire Lagan. For a fit party of climbers it is perfectly feasible in a summer's day to leave Loch Coruisk using this route to gain Coire Lagan, do a climb, and return to Coruisk by nightfall. About 5000 ft. of climbing are involved.

COIRE AN LOCHAIN AND
COIRE A CHAORUINN

---

(1) **Sgurr Dubh Mor** 3096 ft.
(2) **Sgurr Dubh na da Bheinn** 3078 ft.
(3) **Sgurr Coire an Lochain** 2491 ft.
(4) **Sgurr Thearlaich** 3208 ft.

Coir a' Chaoruinn is a shallow corrie that is cradled in the arms of the Sgurr Dubhs, between the north side of the Beag and the east side of the Mor. It is the best route to Coire an Lochain. The entrance is guarded by slabs, but thereafter there is no difficulty. It holds snow well, and is a pleasant route to the col between Sgurr Dubh Beag and Mor under firm winter conditions. As one walks northward along the shore to Loch Coruisk a steep white waterslide marks the entrance.

Coire an Lochain is a superbly wild corrie surrounded by fine peaks. From Coruisk hut it is gained by entering Coire a' Chaoruinn and traversing in by one of two rakes. At 800 ft. a broad horizontal grass rake leads into the lower part of Coire an Lochain, at a height convenient for climbs on the east flank. At 1300 ft. an ascending narrow rake, well cairned, leads into the upper corrie below the lochan. The lower end of this rake is marked by an arch formed by a large tilted slab. The upper end of the route is marked by a prominent isolated stone with a cairn on it some 200 ft. below the lochan. Alternatively one can tramp another half mile up the boggy meadows at the head of Loch Coruisk, one of the wildest spots in the world, and then follow the burn issuing from the corrie. As the name implies, there is a lochan at 1900 ft. cupped in a shelf. The low point at the head of the corrie is at 2806 ft., the Bealach Coire an Lochain, and provides a route to Coire a' Ghrunnda and to the Bealach Mhic Coinnich. These ascents are rough, but without technical difficulty.

Sgurr Coire an Lochan (2491 ft. Peak of the Corrie of the Lochan)

This fine summit is unlikely to be climbed for its own sake. On its east and north flanks it has impressive crags. These bear few climbs probably because they lack natural lines. When on the face the atmosphere is one of big mountaineering. The lie of the rock is against the climber, and it oozes moisture. Seen from the corrie the eastern edge shows in profile with a large overhang at its base. *Raeburn's* route (1000 ft. V.D.) starts here, eventually traversing onto the eastern face. The face has never been climbed direct, but devious routes have been made up it.

The north summit (2398 ft.) is connected to the main peak by a deep gap (2336 ft.) whose passage involves some rock-climbing. The peak is said to have been climbed first by Naismith, Howell and Collie with the guide McKenzie in 1896.

Sgurr Thearlaich (3208 ft. Charles' Peak), see also Coire Lagan [11, 12]

This fine narrow summit is not a Munro in its own right, being too close to higher things. It was unnamed when the S.M.C. ancients first came to the Cuillin, and was named after Charles (Thearlaich) Pilkington, then president of the Alpine Club. On the Coire an Lochain side there is a steep but broken buttress, first climbed by Raeburn in 1913. Left of this it throws down some very steep rock. Following the ridge southwards towards Sgurr Dubh one quickly arrives at one of the Cuillin main ridge's principal traps – the Thearlaich-Dubh gap (2950 ft.). This formidable cleft has nearly vertical walls 80 ft. high on the north side, and 30 ft. to the south. It is worth recalling the unintentional humour of the first edition –

'It is recommended that a party of tourists should not all descend into the gap at the same time in case they might have to remain there permanently.'

In fact the 80 ft. wall is a chimney climb that was originally about difficult standard, but polished through use has become V.D. The south side is a good deal harder. The gap itself may be escaped from on the Ghrunnda side by moderate climbing, but the Coire an Lochain side reveals nothing but a yawning abyss. The gap was first crossed by N. Collie and W. W. King in 1891.

The south wall of the gap is in fact a pinnacle, and a further descent has then to be made to Bealach Coire an Lochain (2806 ft.), an easy pass already referred to in this section.

The main ridge of this mountain running N.N.W./S.S.E., is a spine of good clean rock, of no difficulty. If one is intent on climbing Sgurr Alaisdair (as one would on a main ridge walk), one can easily gain this peak from the gentle scree slope immediately to the west of the summit ridge.

Sgurr Dubh na da Bheinn

See An Garbh Choire. [2]

Sgurr Dubh Mor

See An Garbh Choire [2]. The north flank of this peak faces on to the corrie and is very steep, though an easy way can be found through the rocks. The N.E. ridge, seen from here in profile looks a most attractive climb, with its overlaps clearly visible.

SECTION 4

COIREACHAN RUADHA

(1)	**Sgurr Mhic Coinnich**	3111 ft.
(2)	**An Stac**	3125 ft.
(3)	**Sgurr Dearg**	3234 ft.
(4)	**Sgurr Banachdich**	3166 ft.
(5)	**Sgurr Thormaid**	3040 ft.
(6)	**Sgurr Ghreadaidh**	3192 ft.
(7)	**Sgurr Coire an Lochain**	2491 ft.

Coireachan Ruadha (Red corries) is one of the remotest corries, and from the point of view of rock-climbing, one of the finest. Isolated buttresses and walls crop up here and there, and it is all sound rock. For the purposes of this guide the limits will be taken on the south by Sgurr Coire an Lochain, and on the north by the east spur of Sgurr a' Ghreadaidh. From Coruisk there are two access routes depending on whether one is making for cliffs of Mhic Coinnich or for more northerly or lower crags. For the former, approach via Coire an Lochain (which see), and for the latter walk a mile past the head of Loch Coruisk and ascend. The going is rough but without technical difficulty. There are three well-known cols, the Bealach Banachdich, leading to Glen Brittle, held by many to be the fastest route from Coruisk to Brittle, and the Bealach Mhic Coinnich, and the Bealach Coire Lagan.

Sgurr Mhic Coinnich (3111 ft. McKenzie's Peak), see also Coire Lagan [11]

This peak is one of the sheerest in the Cuillin. The first recorded ascent of the then nameless peak was by Charles Pilkington of the A.C., accompanied by his guide, John McKenzie. Scotland is fortunate that in those days there were men at large sensitive to their environment. It was no time before the peak was known by its Gaelic form, Sgurr Mhic Coinnich.

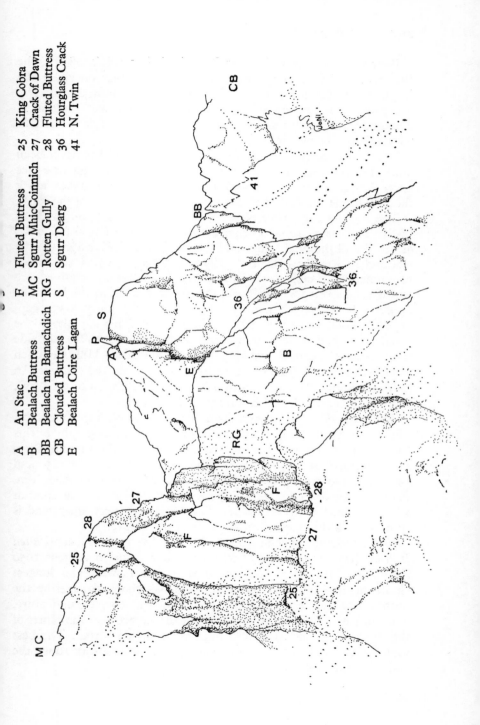

MC

A   An Stac
B   Bealach Buttress
BB   Bealach na Banachdich
CB   Clouded Buttress
E   Bealach Coire Lagan

F   Fluted Buttress
MC Sgurr MhicCoinnich
RG Rotten Gully
S   Sgurr Dearg

25 King Cobra
27 Crack of Dawn
28 Fluted Buttress
36 Hourglass Crack
41 N. Twin

Between this peak and Sgurr Thearlaich is a col (2928 ft.), the Bealach Mhic Coinnich, accessible to the scrambler on either the Lagan or the Coruisk side. On the latter side it is best ascended by first gaining the col between Sgurr Coire an Lochain and Thearlaich. The gully leading to the col is marked by a rib of rock to the left, which should be avoided.

The direct ascent of Mhic Coinnich from this col has never been done. It overhangs. All routes traverse on to the Lagan face (see Coire Lagan). Sgurr Thearlaich presents no difficulty taken along the crest from the col, though there is an awkward section at the start. The summit ridge runs N.W./S.E. It is sound rock, not serrated badly. The easiest route is from the Bealach Coire Lagan (2690 ft.) at the foot of the N.W. ridge and thence up the N.W. ridge. On the Coireachan Ruadha side, the gully which leads to this col is not recommended, being steep and slabby. The descent requires care and is unpleasant for 400 ft. On this descent, hold to the left. The Lagan side is easy, if penitential. There is a slightly lower gap, 2639 ft., lying 120 yards S.E. of the real col. This gap should be avoided as a way of ascent or descent. On the Coireachan Ruadha side the peak may be gained by taking the route to Bealach Mhic Coinnich as far as the base of the steep buttress falling from the summit. An easy ascending rake runs rightwards across the face on to the N.W. summit ridge, which is then turned and climbed.

The east side of the mountain harbours some superb climbs. Fig. 3 and Photo 21 gives an idea of the complex topography of this face. There is an upper tier of rocks that finish on the summit ridge, a vast terrace, and lower rocks. The first climbs done in 1950 and 1951 are due to W. D. Booker and C. M. Dixon of Aberdeen. *Forgotten Groove* (250 ft. V.D.) goes vertically up to the summit as the summit buttress. On its lower part it is very steep, and is climbed by a thin crack in the corner of the groove.

Far to the right, finishing on the N.W. ridge, is the superb *Fluted Buttress* [route 28], whose first ascent they made in August 1950 (photo 21). It was at the time one of the hardest and longest climbs in the Cuillin. A series of overhangs about 200 feet up the buttress, broken into three fins, or flutes, is a conspicuous feature. The start of the climb is at a cairn on the terrace near the centre of the buttress, to the right of a huge right angled corner. The best route is not easy to follow, and though there is an escape route, the climb is of sustained severity.

11. Cuillin cottage, Glenn Brittle.

12. Looking up Loch Coruisk from Sgurr na Stri to the Cuillin Ridge, with Sgurr a'Ghreadaidh and Sgurr a'Mhadaidh above the head of the loch.

Crack of Dawn [27] lies to the left, equally hard, and crosses *Fluted Buttress.* Then in 1960 C. J. S. Bonnington and T. W. Patey made a direct route up the face starting from the bay on the left of *Crack of Dawn* (*King Cobra* 700 ft., V.S. 25). Though these climbs are very fine they require considerable effort to reach them, and more important, their orientation means that they catch sun only in the morning and dry out slowly.

To the north of the 2639 ft. col is a fine buttress that culminates on the main ridge between 2639 ft. col and the Bealach Coire Lagan (2695 ft.). Called Bealach Buttress, it has been the setting for several very fine climbs of which *'Hour Glass Crack'* (V.S. 36), *'Black Cleft'* (V.S.), and *'Thunderbolt Shelf'* (V.D.) may be recommended. All these climbs start from Rotten Gully, near the base of the buttress. (Fig. 3).

An Stac (3125 ft. the stack), see also Coire Lagan

This is less a peak than a knobbly spur on the ridge between Bealach Coire Lagan and Sgurr Dearg. It looks magnificent when seen from the south-east.

From the Bealach (2690 ft.) the spine of An Stac is immediately before one, a crest of rock which would be delightful were the rock not so shattered. This discomfort can be exchanged for the screes to the left hand (S.W.) side. Though rocks of impressive steepness fall to the Coireachan Ruadha side, their friable nature has deterred climbers. However see Sgurr Dearg.

Sgurr Dearg (3209 ft. Red Peak), see also Coire Lagan and Coire Banachdich [10, 11]

The name 'Red Peak' is a Gaelic fantasy, for the most that can be said is that the rock is of a lighter hue than the usual black gabbro. Sgurr Dearg would be the least interesting peak in the Cuillin were it not for the absurd excresence of its S.E. flank, a narrow flake of gabbro that has worn better than its neighbouring rocks, fancifully called the 'Inaccessible Pinnacle'.

Stepping off An Stac, there is a slight dip of 30 ft., and an easy climb to the Sgurr Dearg plateau, with the Inaccessible Pinnacle's long east side immediately in front of one. The Pinnacle (3234 ft.) is higher than the main peak (3209 ft.), and was first climbed by the Pilkington brothers in 1886 by the eastern side. Though moderate in standard, it is remarkably exposed, narrow, totally devoid of belays and has few positive handholds. It is no place for those oppressed by a sense of exposure. The west side is short (40 ft.), but technically harder. The only real difficulty consists in getting from a narrow ledge up a 5 foot rise to a sloping platform, rather slippery when wet. From the platform to the tip of the pinnacle is no problem. On the descent the last man can be secured by slipping the rope round the back of an upright slab.

Naturally an obelisk of this nature upon so easy a mountain had long held fascination for native and stranger alike. Pilkington's account in Alpine Journal (vol. xiii) may interest readers:

'The pinnacle had attracted much attention in the district, and had often been attacked by local climbers; but it deserved its name of Inaccessible till 1880, when my brother and I climbed it by its east edge. The following year a shepherd got up, after having taken off his shoes. It was then unclimbed until Walker, Hulton, and my brother made the third ascent in 1883, since which date it has been ascended several times. In 1886 Mr. A. H. Stocker and Mr. A. G. Parker climbed it by the western end. Desirous of following their example, and having reached this end of the rock, we asked Mackenzie, who had come with us to carry the camera, if he would like to go with us. He had done it from the other side before. "Oh, yes," was his ready reply. Off went his boots, and we tied him on to the rope. I believe his great anxiety for some time had been that we might send him round with the luggage to the other side and not give him a chance of the climb. The first few steps were easy. We then traversed a little ledge, about 6 inches wide, to our left, leading on to the north face for about 20 feet. As we stood in turn upon the highest part of this ledge (it descended a little beyond) a smooth, slanting rock came down, its edge ending about half-way up to our chests.

'The next step, or wriggle, was the difficulty. It would have been fairly easy had the standing place been firm and good, but it was a narrow piece of hard, slippery trap, and shook slightly when tried with a stock. We slowly and steadily drew ourselves up till we landed flat on the steep, smooth incline above. Very steep and smooth it was, and care was required as we wormed ourselves up for about 10 feet, till we found on the left a good crack large enough for our fingers. The difficulties were over when that was accomplished, for a few changes of hand along this ledge slid us under a rough, upright rock, a swarm up which landed us on good holding ground on the west end of the pinnacle, and about 40 feet from its base, whence two minutes' pleasant scramble took us past the extraordinary bolster stone of the highest point beyond.

'We descended by the east edge, which we found easier than we expected. No doubt it was easier now; for on the first ascent very great care and labour were required to pull out stones, loose, but still forming part of the natural rock, and often the whole edge, which, by the way, is only six inches to a foot wide in many places. Of the two routes, the west is the shortest and most difficult, the east is the longest, the finest, and most sensational; both require care, and a slip from the east end would be fatal' (*Alpine Journal*, vol. xiii).

In winter clad in an ice armour, the pinnacle begins to live up to its name. Harold Raeburn, however, overcame even that long before the era of short axes.

As far back as 1912 (*Julian's route* V.D.), the Coireachan Ruadha face was climbed no further explorations have been reported, but would seem possible. The easiest access is to traverse from the Bealach Coire na Banachdich at the level of the screes.

Sgurr Banachdich (3166 ft.), see also Coire Banachdich [10]

There is more than usual doubt as to the meaning of this name. Some says it means 'small-pox peak' justifying this by pointing to the peculiar rock formation in the corrie of the same name. The name Sgurr na Banachaig was also known locally, meaning 'milk-maid's peak', and certainly remains of summer shielings are to be found in the corrie, and the upper pastures are good.

The peak has four summits, three over three thousand feet. They are separated from Sgurr Dearg by an easy ridge, and for this reason are hard to follow in mist. The Bealach Coire na Banachdich (2791 ft.) is straightforward on the Coruisk side. It is probably the easiest pass in the Cuillin. Nevertheless on the Glen Brittle side the way is not obvious. Many people consider it the fastest route from Glen Brittle to Coruisk Hut.

The first peak above the Bealach is an unnamed top at 2887 ft. from which a spur (Sron Buidhe) runs E.N.E. dividing Coireachan Ruadha into two units. If one wishes to make the ascent of Banachdich from the east side, Sron Buidhe provides the most interesting approach, short of rock climbing.

The Coireachan Ruadha face sports several medium length climbs, pioneered by Brooker and Patey. Just north of the Bealach is a buttress divided by a dark gully – The Twins. The *south twin* is an M.D. of 250 ft., climbed on the ridge edge. The *north twin* is M.S. 300 ft. [41, Fig. 3].

Beyond Sron Buidhe a further dip of 2845 ft. provides another possible pass. A descent to the corrie here leads to the base of a summit cliff and Midget ridge, 400 ft. Yet further north a prominent buttress (*Clouded Buttress*, Fig. 3) gave Patey and Booker a 600 ft. M.S. Above to the north is the third top, 3023 ft., followed after a shallow dip by the second top (3089 ft.) and another little dip to the main top at 3166 ft.

This peak is a fine viewpoint, a place from which to ponder the Cuillin north and southwards, where one may, without getting off one's niche amongst the rocks, gaze down to the gloomy recess of the great corrie of water (Coruisk) below one, peer over Druim nan Ramh to the Red Cuillin, and if one is doing the main ridge, congratulate oneself on reaching the halfway mark.

Sgurr Thormaid (3040 ft.) see also Coire nan Eich and Coire a' Ghreadaidh. [9]

By naming this eminence Norman's peak, after the great Norman Collie, it has been elevated from its former second class status as the North top of Banachdich. Its traverse offers no difficulty. On the Banachdich side there is a col at 2914 ft., gained by rough unstable scree from Coireachan Rudha. Beyond, to the north between it and Sgurr a' Ghreadaidh is no more than a dip. Its steep eastern rocks yielded their first climb, *Peridot* 700 ft. V.S., only in 1968. It takes the easiest line.

Sgurr a' Ghreadaidh (3192 ft.) see also Coire a' Ghreadaidh [9]

The meaning of this name is uncertain. 'Peak of the Thrashings' is one possibility if for thrashings one equates mighty winds. The peak rises boldly at the head of Coruisk, presenting precipices whose first impact on the climbers is tremendous. However, on closer inspection its huge south wall turns out to be less continuous and less steep than supposed. The summit ridge is narrow, but without difficulty. The view down Loch Coruisk is worth any effort. There are two summits, the northernmost being the higher.

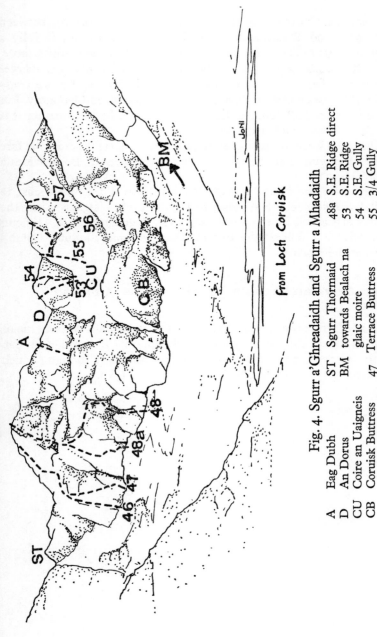

Fig. 4. Sgurr a'Ghreadaidh and Sgurr a Mhadaidh.

from Loch Coruisk

A	Eag Dubh	ST	Sgurr Thormaid
D	An Dorus	BM	towards Bealach na
CU	Coire an Uaigneis		glaic moire
CB	Coruisk Buttress	47	Terrace Buttress
	Sgurr a'Ghreadaidh	46	Terrace Gully
	Sgurra a' Mhadaidh	48	S.E. Ridge

48a	S.E. Ridge direct
53	S.E. Ridge
54	S.E. Gully
55	3/4 Gully
56	2/3 Gully
57	1/2 Gully

From the Coruisk side the easy approach is to the col between Thormaid and Banachdich, of which the final section is fully a thousand feet of scree. Fig. 4 shows the layout of the Coruisk face.

To the S.S.E. of the peak stands a low buttress that later merges with the S. face. It is cut by a deep gully, known as *Terrace Gully* (V.D. 46), first climbed in 1920 by Steeple, Barlow, and Doughty. For those who like gully climbs, this is a fine route. In wet weather it is the channel for much water.

The gully butts on to a great terrace that cuts right across the face of the mountain at about 1500 ft. The buttress itself also provides a climb (D. 47).

Further to the right Menzies and Morrison did a direct start to Collie's *S.E. ridge* climb 48, described under Coire Uaigneis. Since the climb starts about 1150 ft. above sea level, the route is long. Difficult in standard, it follows the line of least resistance, joining Collie's climb at the terrace.

Sgurr Coire an Lochain (2491 ft.) see also Coire an Lochain [3].

The N.E. face is a complex mass of short steep walls without major features, except the great vertical section opposite Bidean Druim nan Ramh. There is here a line of weakness from left to right which permits a climb of about 400 ft. (*Shelf Route*, M.S.).

COIRE AN UAIGNEIS

---

(1) **Sgurr a' Ghreadaidh**   3192 ft.
(2) **Sgurr a Mhadaidh**   3012 ft.
(3) **Bidean Druim nan Ramh** 2850 ft.

Properly speaking one must climb out of Coireachan Ruadha to gain this little high corrie situated under Sgurr a' Ghreadaidh and Mhadaidh. Not even much of a burn runs out of it. Related to it on the right or east is the Glaic Moire (Great Hollow) to the east of which rises the long long ridge of Druim nan Ramh. The col at the top of the Glaic Moire is a simple way of crossing the Cuillin, but since it lands one far from either Glen Brittle or Sligachan, it is little used... See Fig. 6, p. 117.

Sgurr a' Ghreadaidh (3192 ft.)

See Coireachan Ruadha for full details and also Coire a' Ghreadaidh. The N.E. face of this peak falls into Coire an Uaigneis. One climb of no great moment but of great delight is Collie's S.E. ridge (D.48) which is on bald rock for about 2500 ft., making it the longest climb of its standard in the country. The route lies over slabs on the south-west side of a small stream coming from the corrie. In due course it leads leftwards on to the precipitous face overlooking Coireachan Ruadha (see Fig. 4, Section 4). The upper part of the face is cut off from the lower by overhanging walls, to evade which one must hold to the left.

Coruisk Buttress (600 ft. S.) (C.B., Fig. 4) is an isolated rock mass, topped by slab. It is the lowest rock in the corrie. The climb starts right of Collie's route. A single line of weakness runs upwards obliquely from left to right and determines the route. The route of high angle and continuous difficulty.

Sgurr a Mhadaidh (3012 ft.), see also Coire a Mhadaidh [8]

The traverse of this summit involves a measure of rock climbing.

It is well defended by cliffs on both sides. Between it and Ghreadaidh is the col known as An Dorus, the door. On the Coruisk side this col is a difficult gully for 200 ft. The mountain has four peaks separated by shallow dips. The S.W. is the highest. The compass reads very erratically on this peak. There are several climbs on the Uaigneis face (Fig. 4, Section 4). The S.E. buttress of the southernmost peak is obvious when approaching from the Coruisk side. A gully splits it in two, and an excellent 800 ft. climb (D. 54) was made on the west side of the gully in 1897 by a party led by William Brown. This gully itself has also been climbed, as have all the others on this face.

Bidean Druim nan Ramh (2850 ft. Ridged Peak of the Oars), see also Tarneilear and Harta Corries. [6, 8]

This tiny three pronged peak may lack the elevation of a Munro, but lacks nothing else. The summits are pure sound rock, and a delight to straddle.

The main Cuillin ridge bends sharply about the central (highest) peak from south to west. A certain amount of climbing is involved even in the normal traverse, and on the north side of the central peak is an overhang. A traverse on the west side avoids this, but it is more interesting to scale the short vertical wall on the east side of the gap, and rejoin the crest above the overhang.

Between Sgurr a' Mhadaidh and this peak is the Bealach na Glaic Moire (2492 ft.), an easy pass, with water not too far down the north side. This is a major Cuillin pass, and its ascent in mist is confusing. From Loch Coruisk head follow the main river bed. Fig 4. Where it forks left, even if that branch looks bigger, ignore it. The true burn peters out in a scree some 500 ft. from the col, and the best line is on the rock and grass to the left (south) of the scree.

Running south-east from the central peak is a fine ridge, called Druim nan Ramh, that is "Ridge of the Oars", presumably a tribute to its serrated nature. Though the climbing is moderate, it makes a delightful approach to the peak. Druim nan Ramh runs right back almost to the mouth of Loch Coruisk, on the north-east side, thus giving almost 4 miles of elevated ridge walking of an interesting nature. There are continually changing views of the Cuillin to the west and ahead, towards Blaven to the east, and later down into the solitude of Harta Corrie.

Above Loch Coruisk, Druim nan Ramh, at that point an almost

13. Camping beside Loch Scavaig. The 'Mad Burn' is across the
water and above the hollow Caisteal an garbh choire.

14. Sailing to Loch Coruisk in May; the Cuillins have a powder of new snow on them.

15. The ' bad step ' on the coastal path between Loch Coruisk and Camasunary.

16. Loch Coruisk. Right to left: Druim nan Ramh, Bidein Druim nan Ramh, Sgurr a'Mhadaidh. The distant corrie is Coire Uagneis. The Bealach na glaic moire lies to the left of Bidein Druim nan Ramh.

17. Sgurr na Stri from the main Cuillin ridge. Elgol is on the nearer peninsula.

18.   On the crest of the Cuillin ridge, Garsbheinn in the distance, the most southerly point of the Ridge.

19. Garsbheinn and Sgurr a'choire bhig from Sgurr nan Eag.

20. Sgurr Dubh Mor from Sgurr a'choire lochan. The intervening corrie is Coire a'Chaoruinn.

level ridge 1700 ft. high, presents a rocky west face with two prominent buttresses, steepest at the base, (see photos 16 and 12). The difficulties are neither so great nor so continuous as they look, and though there are routes of Very Difficult and Severe, in general the standard is a little lower, and the competent party can move almost at will over the upper part of the face. (See also Coir' Uisg [1]).

At the head of Coruisk there is a saddle on Druim nan Ramh (1500 ft.). On the Coruisk side it is littered with crags, but careful scouting can reveal a walking route up and down. This route can be used in approaching Harta and Lota corrie from Coruisk.

HARTA AND LOTA CORRIES

(1)	**Bidelin Druim nan Ramh**	2850 ft.
(2)	**An Caisteal**	2724 ft.
(3)	**Sgurr na Bhairnich**	2826 ft.
(4)	**Bruach na Frithe**	3143 ft.
(5)	**Sgurr a Fionn Choire**	3068 ft.
(6)	**Am Basteir**	3069 ft.
(7)	**Sgurr nan Gillean**	3167 ft.
(8)	**Sgurr na h-Uamha**	2416 ft.
(9)	**Druim Hain and Meall Dearg**	1200 ft. approx.

Due south from Sligachan runs Glen Sligachan. A vestigial path among the bogs on the east side of the river runs to Camusunary and in an hour and a half leads to the Lochan Dubha below the west flanks of Marsco. Already at this point the main stream of the river has turned westwards into Harta Corrie. To the north is a rocky escarpment, untracked, with deep tussocky grass. The going is heavy. Yet the very loneliness of the situation is a sufficient compensation. Just under Meall Dearg is a large boulder (Bloody Stone) which offers some shelter and interesting rock gymnastics. In its upper reaches the corrie splits into three small corries, of which Lota Corrie is the largest and finest. In the normal course of events walkers and climbers are not attracted by the long haul up to these corries via Glen Sligachan, though a descent is common enough. Upper Harta Corrie is accessible in $2\frac{1}{2}$ hours from Coruisk via the saddle on Druim nan Ramh. (See Coire Uaigneis [5]).

Bidein Druim nan Ramh (2850 ft.), see also Corrie Uaigneis and Tarneilear. [5, 8]

The centre and north peaks of this mountain present flanks to Harta Corrie which are short but steep. Immediately north of the north peak is a col (2494 ft.), easily passed on either the Harta or Tarneilear side, which provides easy access to the main peak.

An Caisteal (2724 ft. The Castle), see also Tarneilear [8].
Sgurr na Bhairnich (2826 ft. The Limpet)

These two points are simply major excrescences on the ridge between Bruach na Frithe and Bidein Druim nan Ramh, having a deep gash between them. There is no difficulty in following their crest, but coming from the south the ridge walker often misses the true track, and keeps to the crest of Caisteal too long, finding himself overlooking a sizeable abyss above Harta Corrie. It is wiser not to scramble down, but to return to the point where the track takes to the west side.

The Harta face of An Caisteal is of considerable interest to climbers. Two large gullies split the face into three buttresses, all climbed, each long (over 1000 ft.), steep, and often slabby. The easiest lines are about Difficult, and were first essayed by Harold Raeburn in 1905. The gullies have some very difficult moves in them.

The gap between Caisteal and Bhairnich is an impressive cleft, offering coolness on the warmest Cuillin heatwave. Harta Corrie is accessible with difficulty. From the east side of the gully a traverse of a short rock wall takes one on to the screes, just above a point where the gully plunges steeply.

Sgurr na Bhairnich is without rock-climbing interest.

Bruach na Frithe (3143 ft. The Brae of the Forest), see also Fionn Choire and Tarneilear. [7, 8]

This might be described as the safest of the Cuillin hills and the only one open to the pure walker. Its flanks are almost totally devoid of steep rock, yet its summit is shapely enough. The main ridge at this point turns from N.N.E. to east-west. Screes run down to Lota Corrie, and the gap between it and Sgurr na Bhairnich is without difficulty. As a view-point for the Cuillin it is magnificent, but one would hardly choose to approach from the Lota Corrie side.

Sgurr a Fionn Choire (3068 ft. Peak of the Fair Corrie), see also Coire a Bhasteir. [7, 8]

A short dip at 2964 ft. separates this spur from the Bruach na Frithe. Beyond the peak to the east is a significant pass, the Bealach nan Lice (2940 ft.), Pass of the Flat Stones, easy, linking Lota and Fionn Corries. A small steep buttress stands at the end of the col.

Am Bhasteir (3069 ft. The Executioner), see also Coire an Bhasteir. [7]

This peak is outshone by the spectacular axe head of rock immediately below and to the west of it, Bhasteir Tooth (3005 ft.). It was first climbed by Collie in 1889 from the Lota Corrie side. This route involves traversing from the Belach nan Lice. Keep close to the rocks until almost at the lowest point of the rocks. Start climbing on a westward traverse (M.D.).

This descent into Lota Corrie can be avoided using Naismith's route (D.) on the S.W. face of the tooth. From the neck at the base of the tooth (west side) climb easy rocks (trending rightwards) to a horizontal ledge with a large stone lying on it. From the end of the ledge a 15 ft. face is climbed on indifferent holds leading to the base of a chimney with good belay. 20 ft. up the chimney a jammed block is passed and a rightward slanting crack with excellent holds leads one on the roof of the tooth. The route does not appear as an obvious easy line.

The ascent of Am Bhasteir from here is about 80 ft., and involves overcoming a short overhang. On this face it is more usual to descend from Am Bhasteir to the tooth, either on rappel or hitching the rope for the overhang.

Am Bhasteir itself is a walk taken from the east side, where the Bealach a' Bhasteir forms an easy pass between Lota and Coire a' Bhasteir.

Lota Corrie at this point is steep, and one looks down to its lip where lush mosses and grass ooze cool and fragrant water.

Sgurr nan Gillean (3167 ft. The Peak of the Young Men), see also Coire a Bhasteir. [7]

This mountain will be described in detail under Corrie a' Bhasteir. Its west ridge from Bealach a' Bhasteir throws down difficulties but no challenge on the Lota side. Southwards from the summit a long graceful spur descends to 2099 ft., and rises again to 2416 ft. at Sgurr na h-Uamha. This ridge is a worthy finish to the Cuillin main ridge walk.

Sgurr na h-Uamha (2416 ft. Peak of the Cave).

This acute summit as a vantage point from which to meditate, has no equal. The flanks of the peak are steep with slabs of fine gabbro.

The S.W. face offers many climbs. It is divided into three distinct tiers, and though quite long routes from Difficult to Severe have been recorded, the climbs lack true continuity. The upper tier is the only true buttress and spreads round to the east side of the peak, and is the location of a number of new rock routes. On descent, if heading for Loch Coruisk, it is better to head westerly first, into Lota Corrie, while, if aiming at Sligachan, return to the col with Gillean and drop into the Coire nan Allt Geala.

If ascending from Sligachan some sporting routes offering a lot of scrambling may be found on the Glen Sligachan flank of the mountain.

Druim Hain and Meall Dearg [1200 ft. approx.]

These two names are given to rocky but indefinite eminences at the head of Glen Sligachan. They are littered with rocks and outcrops and boiler-plate slabs both to north and south. The best route between Coruisk and Harta Corrie is between Druim Hain and Druim nan Ramh, dropping into Coire Riabhach (path down to Coruisk). See also Strathaird.

SECTION 7

SLIGACHAN CORRIES

---

(1)	**Nead na h-Iolaire**	850 ft.
(2)	**Sgurr nan Gillean**	3167 ft.
(3)	**Am Bhasteir**	3069 ft.
(4)	**Sgurr a' Bhasteir**	2951 ft.
(5)	**Bruach na Frithe**	3143 ft.

The Sligachan corries comprise from east to west: Coire Riabhach, Coire a' Bhasteir, Fionn Choire. The latter is hidden behind Sgurr a' Bhasteir, and is not visible from Sligachan. Here, uniquely in the Cuillins, a foreground of moor gives a perspective to the mountains, and Sgurr nan Gillean looks twice its height. Under a mantle of snow (see cover photo) or in spring when the corries are snow filled Sgurr nan Gillean is one of the finest sights in Scotland, and even the scree-ridden Sgurr a' Bhasteir is briefly elevated to the peerage. There is no totally safe route to the summit for the walker unacquainted with rocks, and the intervening peat hags have claimed more than one victim desperately trying to find a way home in mist.

Coire Riabhach contains two lochans, and some scattered small crags above it. Coire a' Bhasteir is an impressive place with fine rock scenery. The lower corrie reveals glaciated slabs, and the river, the Allt Beag, has cut a deep gorge. Higher up there is a small lochan, but such is the rocky and scree-ridden nature of the setting, that few plants can grow. The simplest access is to cross the Allt Dearg by the bridge 200 yards from the hotel, and strike across the pathless moor. Once on the west bank of the gorge, cairns will be found and the path re-appears. The coire may be ascended without technical difficulty, but it is rough and tedious going.

Fionn Choire lies to the west of Sgurr a' Bhasteir, and is gained by taking the Glen Brittle path towards the Bealach a' Mhaim. See Sgurr a' Fionn Choire.

Nead na h-Iolaire (approx. 900 ft., Nest of the Eagles).

This black crag sits low on the flanks of Gillean two miles due north of Sligachan. It has several rock routes to entertain the off-day climbers, some as long as 300 ft. It is gained by crossing the Allt Dearg (Red Burn). There is a bridge two hundred yards from the hotel.

Sgurr nan Gillean (3167 ft. Peak of the Young Men), see also Harta Corrie. [6]

The easiest route up this peak, the so-called tourist route, passes to the left of Nead na h-Iolaire (see above) to gain the lochan at the foot of Coire Riabhach, a shallow corrie formed in the N.E. slopes of the mountain proper. The objective is to hit the S.E. ridge of the mountain some 700 ft. below the summit. The route is scree, tedious, but without rock-climbing till the last 500 ft. of the S.E. ridge. However, though the S.E. ridge is the easiest of the ridges of Gillean, it is steep. In general it is easiest on the Lota Corrie side, but if a descent is being made that way in mist great care should be taken not to miss the ridge proper, and so be diverted into Lota Corrie. It is a long road home. On the descent use a compass to keep to the ridge (due east). As soon as the ridge starts to level out to an angle of about 15° or so, turn left (north).

The classic route on Gillean is the pinnacle ridge, that is the north ridge. From Sligachan the four pinnacles are seen end on and cannot be distinguished from each other. They are seen to perfection on the Bealach a' Mhaim path to Glen Brittle or the road from Drynoch.

The first pinnacle is at 2500 ft. (approx.), and may be gained by a scramble from the east having followed the tourist route to the lochans in Coire Riabhach. The Sligachan face has several routes. The latter way suits climbers better since there is more rock-climbing interest. The first pinnacle presents quite a large broken face to the north in two tiers separated by a scree terrace. There are routes on both tiers. The early climbers chose the gullies, finding caves lined with juniper and blaeberries. The cleanest ascent is to hold to Bhasteir Corrie side, and then ascend directly up the west flank. From the first pinnacle to the second, and the second to the third is merely a walk along the ridge, the 'pinnacles', being more apparent than real. Real climbing begins with the third.

The descent of the third pinnacle is tricky. The usual route today (but there are others) is to descend about 30 ft. on the east or Riabhachan side until a cleft with good holds leads down to the right to a shallow gully that leads to the gap between third and fourth pinnacles.

The fourth pinnacle or Knights Peak is steep on the north side, but is easily scaled, and may be turned a little more easily on the Bhasteir side. By continuing the traverse the whole peak is omitted. Due to the proximity of opposing walls of rock, this peak is a great place for echoes. The descent to the neck with the main mountain may be made directly down, though an easier line holds to the Bhasteir side. An easy scree gully leads back in Coire a' Bhasteir.

Beyond the gap is a small tower, easily climbed, and then a direct ascent leads one to the summit by interesting rocks.

The route as a whole is Difficult.

Each of the pinnacles has routes on its west or Bhasteir flank, some of which are very worthwhile. The west face of the main mountain has also fine routes.

The traverse of pinnacles in summer is an exhilarating expedition. In winter it can be magnificent, calling for a very high standard of climbing.

The west ridge of the mountain is heavily used, either by those descending from Gillean by a sporting route, or those completing the ridge walk. From the Bealach a' Bhasteir (2780 ft.) (a walk on both sides) the ridge soars up narrow and dentate, though the only exposed section is at one narrow shattered place where a pinnacle of rock obstructs passage. This is commonly referred to as the Tooth of Gillean or the Gendarme.

Gillean is a magnificent viewpoint for it not only provides a perspective of the Cuillin and the southern sea, but also eastwards up Loch Sligachan, over Raasay, to the great west coast peaks.

Am Bhasteir (3070 ft. The Executioner), see also Harta Corrie [6]

The Coire a' Bhasteir face of this peak is the grander of the two. Though the ascent of the crest from the Bealach a' Bhasteir is without difficulty, interesting possibilities exist on the north face. Fig 5. (Photo 29). The Am Bhasteir chimney may be climbed direct (D93), or alternatively just below a pinnacle on the centre section of the right wall of the chimney, or may traverse right almost to the very west end of the mountain. [94]

21. The Coireachan Rudha face of Sgurr MhicCoinnich. Sgurr Dearg and the Inaccessible Pinnacle beyond.

22. Sgurr MhicCoinnich. The two climbers are descending from Sgurr Thea

23. Early morning sun on the Coruisk slabs of the Dubhs.

24. An Stac Buttress and the Inaccessible Pinnacle from Sgurr Mhic Coinnich

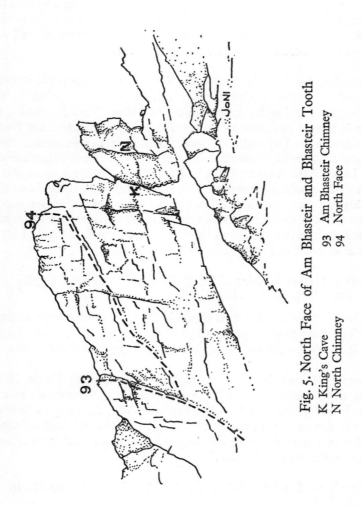

Fig. 5. North Face of Am Bhasteir and Bhasteir Tooth

K King's Cave   93 Am Bhasteir Chimney
N North Chimney   94 North Face

Bhasteir Tooth (3005 ft.), see Harta Corrie. [6]

Two greasy chimney routes will be obvious to anyone who in-
spects this side of the face. That rising to the neck with Am Bhasteir
is called King's Cave, and was one of the earliest routes done, John
McKenzie the guide taking part. The route is subterranean. North

chimney starts to the right of King's, using sloping ledges to gain the chimney. Here there is a small cave, and the climber now faces outwards, and looks for a good handhold high on the outside wall and swings up. There is a thread belay at hand.

Fionn Choire is worth a mention for its charm. Carpeted in grass and wild flowers, it gives easier walking than any other in the Cuillin. It is eminently accessible to the walker from Sligachan, for there is a good path which runs up the N.W. side of the Allt Dearg Mor leaving the Drynoch road some 300 yards above Sligachan. After passing a waterfall, somewhat less than an hour from Sligachan the Allt Dearg Mor is crossed. The Allt a' Fionn Choire is then just to one's right hand. A most useful piece of information is to know that the highest water in the Cuillin exists in this corrie. About 200 ft. below Bealach na Lice some bright green moss marks a little spring (2700 ft.). The descent down this corrie from the Bealach na Lice to Sligachan can be done by a fit man in an hour.

Sgurr a Fionn Choire (3068 ft. Peak of the Fair Corrie), see also Harta Corrie. [6]

A small crag turns towards Bhasteir Corrie, and offers some climbing. The peak may be easily climbed via the Fionn Choire. To the east is the Bealach na Lice (2940 ft.), an easy pass on both sides.

Sgurr a' Bhasteir (2951 ft.) is the spur dividing Fionn Corrie from the Bhasteir Corrie. In a land of rocky peaks this pile of scree is understandably given the cold shoulder. As a way of spinning out the descent on a beautiful evening it has the merit of offering a choice of routes down to the Bhasteir Corrie or back to the main Sligachan/Glen Brittle path.

Bruach na Frithe (3143 ft. Brae of the Forest), see Harta Corrie. [6]

Ascended from Fionn Choire (which see above) this peak is the most straightforward walk in the Cuillin, and no rock-climbing of any sort is involved. For variety the walker would probably ascend by the N.W. ridge and descend by the Fionn Choire, in which case he would keep ascending the Glen Brittle path as far as the Bealach a' Mhaim, the imperceptible watershed between Glen Brittle and

Sligachan. From here a long grassy slope passes a point marked on the O.S. map Tobar nan Uaislean (gentry's well or spring) at a height of 1683 ft.

For the ordinary walker it cannot be stressed too strongly that the difficulties of route finding off Bruach na Frithe in low mist are considerable. As soon as one is down to about 1500 ft. the land becomes featureless. If aiming for Sligachan a safe rule would be to follow the Allt na Fionn Choire, the burn flowing out the Fionn Corrie till one hits the Bealach a' Mhaim path (at about 1800 ft. this burn disappears for a short distance). The party must have a compass, and from the summit one cannot go far wrong if one holds due north till one gains the Fionn Corrie (15 minutes and a descent of several hundred feet), and then swings left on a course of 330° magnetic. Any stream encountered should be flowing in a northerly direction, and if so may be followed. If not one may judge that one has held too much to the west, and not sufficiently to the north. See Photo 25.

If the objective is Tarneilear then leave the summit on a due west tack, even though the initial descent is on steep rough scree. Eventually one is bound to come to the burn flowing out of Tarneilear Corrie, and so down to Glen Brittle.

COIRE NA CREICHE: COIR A' MHADAIDH AND TARNEILEAR

(1)	**Bruach na Frithe**	3143 ft.
(2)	**Sgurr na Bhairnich**	2826 ft.
(3)	**An Caisteal**	2724 ft.
(4)	**Bidein Druim nan Ramh**	2850 ft.
(5)	**Sgurr a' Mhadaidh**	3012 ft.
(6)	**Sgurr Thuilm**	2885 ft.
(7)	**Sgurr an Fheadain**	2125 ft. approx.

Prior to 1965 O.S. maps named the two inner corries wrongly. Coir a' Mhadaidh is in fact under Sgurr a' Mhadaidh. One looks straight into these corries as one drives over the moor into Glen Brittle from Carbost. The waters of Coire na Creiche join those of the Allt a' Mhaim just a few hundred yards above the point where the road meets the river. Separated by the magnificent promontory of Sgurr an Fheadain (the 'Fh' is mute) into Coire a' Mhadaidh and Tarneilear, the name of the main corrie applies to the lower grassy slopes (Fig. 6). There are two waterfalls at about the 500 ft. contour, creating some lovely natural bathing pools. Fig. 6.

Tarneilear (Thunderer) is the more northerly of the two corries. Its left wall is simply the long scree slope of Bruach na Frithe. To the right the rugged rocks of Sgurr au Fheadain rise, without showing much in the way of definite climbs. At the head is Bidein Druim nan Ramh. To the left of this peak is a col (2507 ft.) separating the barely discernible mass of An Caisteal. This col is easy and offers a walk into Harta Corrie. This route offers a walking route to Bruach na Frithe, Bidein Druim nan Ramh and the climbs of the Harta Corrie face of An Caisteal. An easy route to the Bealach na Glaic Moire ascends this corrie then crosses the shoulder of Sgurr an Fheadain. For descriptions of the peaks see Section 6 – HARTA CORRIE.

Coir a' Mhadaidh (Corrie of the Foxes) is a magnificent place

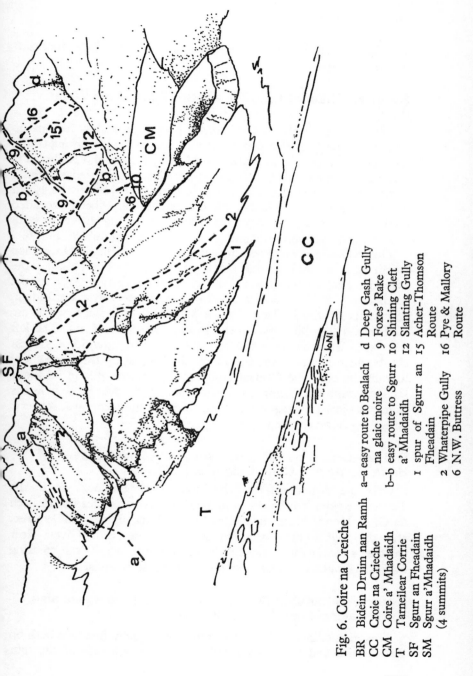

Fig. 6. Coire na Creiche

BR Bidein Druim nan Ramh
CC Croic na Creiche
CM Coire a' Mhadaidh
T   Tarneilear Corrie
SF Sgurr an Fheadain
SM Sgurr a' Mhadaidh
    (4 summits)

a–a easy route to Bealach
     na glaic moire
b–b easy route to Sgurr
     a' Mhadaidh
1 spur of Sgurr an
     Fheadain
2 Whaterpipe Gully
6 N.W. Buttress

d Deep Gash Gully
9 Foxes' Rake
10 Shining Cleft
12 Slanting Gully
15 Acher-Thomson
     Route
16 Pye & Mallory
     Route

117

offering a wealth of climbs and stimulating surroundings. Its head-wall is entirely rock.

Sgurr an Fheadain (2215 ft. approx. Peak of the Water Pipe).

This peak is rarely climbed for its own sake, and is famous on account of the gully that cleaves its west face – the *Waterpipe Gully*. Though first ascended as far back as 1895 by Kelsall and Hallitt, it is a route of considerable difficulty (Severe) and great length, for it comprises 20 pitches, in all some 1300 ft. In wet weather the ascent can be 'monstrous'. Though all the pitches have been ascended directly, in the earlier ascents many were turned on the south wall.

The buttresses on either side give interesting scrambles. Fig. 6.

This peak is properly speaking a western spur of Bidein Druim nan Ramh, and the walk to that summit is pleasant. The tourist route over the Bealach na Glaic Moire to Coruisk in fact goes up the Tarneilear side of Fheadain, crosses the neck between it and Bidein, and heads for the Bealach. On the Mhadaidh side slabs, which are cleft by three gullies, rise to the Bealach na Glaic Moire. The left most seen from below is the North Gully, and provides a modest climb which is a pleasant alternative to slogging up the stone shoot to gain the col. The Central Gully appears impossible in its lower section, while the *South* (M.S.) first led by W. M. McKenzie has some very hard passages and offers some magnificent rock scenery. It has yet to be climbed direct.

Bidean Druim nan Ramh (West Peak 2780 ft.), see Harta Corrie and Coire Uaigneis. [5, 6]

Only the western of the triple tops of Bidein looks on to the Tarneilear side. To the col to immediate west is in face the Bealach na Glaic Moire. From this col to Coir a' Mhadaidh is rubble scree, and thoroughly unpleasant to ascend or descend. Given clear weather a reasonable route can be picked, but in mist the crossing over the shoulder of Fheadain into Tarneilear is advised.

Sgurr a' Mhadaidh (3010 ft. Peak of the Foxes), see also Coire Uaigneis and Coireachan Ruadha.

This mountain has the distinction of an equally fine face both on the Coruisk and the Glen Brittle sides. The traverse of the four summits is a delightful expedition, somewhat easier if taken from south to north. The S.W. peak is the highest. From Coir a' Mhadaidh the easiest route is to make for the col between Mhadaidh and Sgurr Thuilm (2885 ft.), and then to climb the shattered N.E. ridge. It is narrow, and thus easy to follow.

A quicker route is to press into the head of Tarneilear, and then follow a stony rake (*Foxes Rake*, M.) running up the N.E. face of the mountain. It debouches at a broad notch immediately to the right of the highest peak of Mhadaidh, and can thus be easily distinguished as one is approaching up Coire na Creiche. It is not easy to find in mist without some knowledge of the mountain. The route involves very little climbing, but necessitates the ascent of a short chimney near the top. It is the quickest route to the summit from this corrie.

Yet another rake, higher but roughly parallel to the Foxes Rake, known as *Upper Rake* (M.[b,Fig.6]) takes one out on to the summit via the col between the main peak and the 2925 ft. summit.

The compass reads incorrectly on this mountain.

The rock climbs are numerous. N.W. buttress (D.), one of the first to be made (1896) by Collie gives nearly 1200 ft. of climbing in three sections leading to the N. summit of the peak. The middle section offers some interesting moves. The face directly below the main peak is the steepest and contains several routes of which '*Shining Cleft*', 900 ft. S., can be recommended. All of the gullies, of course, provide routes, some quite hard.

Sgurr Thuilm (2885 ft. Tulin's Peak).

This far-flung northern outrider of Mhadaidh gets scant attention and essentially a nice way home if one wants to keep high as long as possible. It is largely comprised of scree. Photo 32.

COIRE A' GHREADAIDH

---

(1)	**Sgurr Thuilm**	2885 ft.
(2)	**Sgurr a' Ghreadaidh**	3181 ft.
(3)	**An Diollaid**	2375 ft. approx.
(4)	**Sgurr Thormaid**	3040 ft.

The Allt a' Coire Ghreadaidh flows into Glen Brittle past the Youth Hostel. Thus it is one of the most accessible, if not the most prepossessing of Cuillin corries. The N.W. ridge of Sgurr a' Ghreadaidh divides the corrie in two, the northern part being known as Coire an Dorus after the bealach at its head. An Dorus (2779 ft. The Door) lies between Mhadaidh and Ghreadaidh, and was supposed to be the legendary col of the same name used by the McLeods. The earlier S.M.C. guide dismisses this possibility on the grounds that the Coruisk (Coire Uaigneis) side of the col is steep, and requires some climbing, but there is no reason to suppose that skill in climbing started with the advent of the S.M.C. or A.C. The col is a straightforward scree on the west side, and is a narrow gully with several pitches on the Coruisk side. Immediately to its south is a nick in the ridge known as the Eag Dubh (Black Notch, 2890 ft.).

Sgurr Thuilm (2885 ft.), see also Coire a' Mhadaidh. [8]

The south flank of Thuilm is largely scree but it does sport a few outcrops. The lowest of these is a mere 40 minutes walk from the Youth Hostel, and offers a 200 ft. V.S. called *Gail*.

Sgurr a' Ghreadaidh (3181 ft.), see also Coireachan Ruadha and Coire Uaigneis. [4, 5]

On the Coire An Dorus side the peak shows some rock. A 350 foot buttress falls between An Dorus and Eag Dubh, and the N.W. face harbours a 300 foot high band of rocks, of which *Hamish's Chimney* (D.) is about the only recorded route. The N.W. spur itself is open to ascent by a number of ways, those to the south being the harder,

23. The Cuillin Ridge from Bruach na Frithe. The dark peak dominating the distance is Sgurr nan Gillean.

26. Sgurr nan Gillean from Am Bhasteir.

27. The Pinnacle ridge of Sgurr nan Gillean, January 1965.

29. Am Bhasteir from the north, in January.

28. Opposite: The Pinnacle ridge of Sgurr nan Gillean. The lower
Pinnacles I and II are seen as steps on the ridge.

30. Coire nan Creiche from the west. The trident peak to the left is Bidein Druim nan Ramh. To its right is the Bealach na glaic moire, below which is Sgurr an Fheadain. The right-hand

31. Winter traverse, January 1965. Am Bhasteir.

32. Sgurr Thuilm from the north.

and in general a moderate route can be found. The upper point of the spur is called the Sgurr Eadar da Choire, that is the *peak between the corries*.

The crags in the southern of the two corries are much more continuous. There are no simple routes to the main ridge, yet the climbing is not tremendously exciting. *Hidden Gully* (V.D.) cuts obliquely into the mountain, and faces Sgurr Eadar da Choire. It is not apparent till near its foot, and is best located by keeping well up to the left of the coire on the approach. Unlike Hidden Gully, *Vanishing Gully* can be seen (it is well to the right) but peters out on the face in an area of vast slabs (D.).

Sgurr Thormaid (3040 ft.), see also Coireachan Ruadha.

This peak lies in the south corner of the corrie, exciting no great attention. Screes lead up to it, and the traverse of its summit is described in Section 4. It is linked to the west by a spur called An Diollaid.

An Diollaid (The Saddle).

This is not a peak, but the south wall of the corrie. There are two gullies, The obvious one is *Branching Gully* in which the rock scenery is fine. N.E. gully a hundred yards to the left is severe, but the main interest is *Diamond Buttress*, an 800 ft. V.D. taking the line of the buttress immediately to the left of N.E. Gully. An Diollaid is a common and pleasant route of approach to the Banachdich tops, including Sgurr Thormaid.

COIRE NA BANACHDICH
COIRE NAN EICH

(1) **Sgurr nan Gobhar**   2047 ft.
(2) **Sgurr na Banachdich**   3166 ft.
(3) **Sgurr Dearg**   3209 ft.

The minor Coire nan Eich (Corrie of Horses) is a narrow scree cleft between the spur of An Diollaid and the great spur of Sgurr nan Gobhar. Except as an easy way off the ridge it has nothing to recommend it. The Allt Coire na Banachdich flows past Glen Brittle House, and close to the B.M.C. hut. Even in the lower boggy slopes, the track is well enough seen, and is cairned as it enters the corrie. It leads by a tortuous route to the right on the flank of Sgurr Dearg to Bealach Banachdich, which is reckoned one of the easiest routes to Coruisk.

The Coire is spacious, and the head-wall of Banachdich more imposing than serious. It presents a semi-circular wall of rock cut by a deep black gully (*Banachdich Gully*). The rock to either side offers moderate scrambling.

Sgurr nan Gobhar (2047 ft. Peak of the Goats).

This spur offers little more than a route of access or withdrawal from the main ride. The south flank has one prominent gully, of which there is a recorded ascent in 1950. It is very loose, and has little to recommend it.

Sgurr na Banachdich (3166 ft. Smallpox Peak or possible Milk Maid's Peak), see also Coireachan Ruadha. [4]

The north top is the highest of three summits.

The easy ascent is via the Bealach Coire na Banachdich (see above and also Coireachan Ruadha). A pleasant approach is via an Diallaid which coupled with a descent by the Bealach Coire na Banachdich provides a traverse. One can also approach via Sgurr nan Gobhar. The main ridge is delightful and without difficulty. The west wall of the mountain has firm rock, but it is not steep enough for more than interesting scrambling. *Banachdich Gully*, which cleaves the face was climbed by John McKenzie and some clients in 1898 and offers four decent pitches.

Sgurr Dearg (3209 ft. Red Peak), and Inaccessible Pinnacle (3234 ft.), see also Coireachan Ruadha and Coire Lagan. [4, 11]

Perhaps the least spectacular peak in the range, it retains a fascination for everyone on account of the rock plinth on its summit – the Inaccessible Pinnacle.

The easiest route is by the west ridge – a walk. The climber will almost certainly offset this walk by traversing into Coire na Banachdich till at about 1500 ft. he will encounter the *Window Buttress*. Climbed in 1906 by Collie, it is today the most trodden route in Skye. An hour from the Youth Hostel brings one to the rocks, here delightfully sound and clean. The original route (D.) starts at the foot of the rocks and ascends a pinnacle (30 ft.), trends right to a right-angled corner leading to the 'Window'. Thereafter the route goes straight up on excellent rough rock, easing off after about 80 ft. There follows a walk to the summit, beyond which lies the *Inaccessible Pinnacle* (see Coireachan Ruadha and Coire Lagan for details). There are several routes hereabouts.

Further into the corrie on the N.W. slopes of Sgurr Dearg rises another buttress whose base lies about the altitude of the top of Window Buttress, and 400 yards to the left. This is North West Buttress. It is best approached from the corrie, but, of course, may be reached by an uncomfortable scree traverse from the top of Window Buttress. The buttress features two prominent chimneys. The rock is excellent. *Tollie Grooves* (300 ft. S.) starts below the left hand chimney, where it forms a groove. This is climbed. Thereafter the route is tortuous looking for the line of least resistance. *Valkyrie* (300 ft. V.S.). starts 60 ft. to the right of the right hand chimney at a dièdre bounded by a red wall.

COIRE LAGAN

(1)	**Sgurr Dearg**	3209 ft.
(2)	**An Stac**	3125 ft.
(3)	**Sgurr Mhic Coinnich**	3111 ft.
(4)	**Sgurr Thearlaich**	3208 ft.
(5)	**Sgurr Alaisdair**	3257 ft.
(6)	**Sgurr Sgumain**	3108 ft.
(7)	**Sron na Ciche**	2500 ft. approx.

This corrie is the climber's dream come true. It fulfils every require-
ment, aesthetic and technical. Here are the greatest rock faces in the
Cuillin, the most superb juxta-position of buttress and gully, of
cioch and slab, of black rock and blue lochan. The corrie looks west
and north towards the Outer Hebrides. Whether rockwards or seawards, the prospect cannot fail to please. The extent and magnificence of the place is such that not even the noon-day sun in June
completely tames it, and in any other light it is awesome enough. Its
armour of rocks is so rarely pierced that the walker who does not
know the mountains intimately should avoid them in misty weather.
In such conditions even the best climbers may fail to find their peaks
even if they find their routes, and benightment is common enough.
It is a corrie to be treated with respect.

Access to the coire from Glen Brittle ($1\frac{1}{2}/2$ hours) is simple. A track,
or rather series of parallel tracks, leads from the camping ground
or Glen Brittle House over a moor past Lochan an Fhir-Bhallaich, at
which point the cliffs hove in sight. It is a remorseless boggy track,
and in a damp season it is something of a problem to reach the upper
parts of the mountain dry shod.

There are three major cols in the corrie: Bealach Coire Lagan is an
obvious col between An Stac and Sgurr Mhic Coinnich and details
are given below. Bealach Mhic Coinnich is not obvious, but useful,
and is used more often in the reverse direction from Coruisk. Bealach
a' Ghrunnda scarcely appears as a col, though it lies between Sgumain

and Sron na Ciche. It provides a simple exit from Coire a' Ghrunnda, but may be used as a route to Coruisk.

Sgurr Dearg (3209 ft. The Red Peak), see also Coireachan Ruadha and Coire na Banachdich. [4, 10]

The general description of this peak andthe Inaccessible Pinnacle is given in Coireachan Ruadha (Section 4). The Lagan face is largely scree, but enjoys one redeeming feature, the fine South Buttress. Starting some 400 ft. above the Lochan, it provides an interesting route to the Inaccessible Pinnacle. According to the route chosen the standard can vary from Difficult to Severe and is about 300 ft. long. The harder part, which is the lower section, can be avoided by choosing *Baly's* route, that is the gully to the left.

Lower and westwards on the south flank are a number of other small outcrops upon which routes are recorded.

The South face of the Inaccessible Pinnacle faces Coire Lagan. It is a fine vertical wall of sound rock some 100 ft. high, and has naturally attracted many routes. The face is cleaved by a prominent crack, the *South Crack* (V.D.) climbed by Harland in 1906. There are several parallel routes, all V.S.

An Stac (3125 ft. The Stack), see also Coireachan Ruadha. [4]

This peak is no more than the eastern promontory of Sgurr Dearg, and falls in a steep sweet of brittle rocks to Bealach Coire Lagan to the S.E. Though the ascent of this promontory is moderate, the looseness of the holds and the steepness of the ground lend it an uncomfortable feeling of exposure.

It is unlikely anyone is going to climb An Stac for its own sake. The east ridge (M.) is used in any ridge traverse, and very often walkers use the easier line to the south up the parallel scree gully. A crack that cleaves the upper part of the east ridge for 200 ft. offers the most sporting route to the top. There are fine screes for descending the south-side: traverse below the summit over slabs and screes, pass through a nick (cairned) and traverse again to the top of the screes.

Bealach Coire Lagan (2690 ft.), see also Coireachan Ruadha. [4]

This col on the Lagan side is a steep mobile screen run, and while an excellent means of descent makes for a purgatorial ascent. Care should be taken of any parties below one, as some rocks roll far and gather speed here. Care should be taken not to confuse this col with the one 120 yards to the east which though lower (2639 ft.) is not an easy pass on either side. Any climber crossing the main ridge here from Glen Brittle as an approach to Coireachan Ruadha (e.g. to gain Bealach Buttress) may well find his most interesting as well as fastest route is to ascend direct to the 2639 foot col, but it is most definitely not a walker's route.

Sgurr Mhic Coinnich (3111 ft. McKenzie's Peak), also Coireachan Ruadha. [4]

This easiest route up this peak is from the Bealach Coire Lagan and along the narrow but solid crest of the north-west ridge. Traversing from the south (i.e. from Thearlaich), one is faced with a precipitous and unclimbed wall. The simplest way is a ledge that traverses the whole of the S.W. face A-A Fig 7. Known as *Collie's* route (M.) it slants gently upwards until round the buttress and abutting on to the N.W. ridge. A party that wishes to avoid all climbing should drop from the col, and hold to the scree immediately below the rocks, till able to climb up again and regain the main ridge. It is not, however, counselled, and more trouble may be caused than saved, more risk run than avoided. See Fig. 7.

The best, fastest, and traditional route when coming from the south is to follow Collie's ledge for a little distance till a higher ledge appears. Follow this for twenty feet and one finds oneself at the foot of a right-angled open Corner: *King's Chimney* (D.). Though steep it has excellent holds. The overhang is avoided by leading out on to the right wall (60 ft.), thence easy rocks lead to the crest.

The S.W. face of the mountain has one very prominent buttress falling from the summit. Its crest is the *West Buttress* route (D.). *Jeffrey's Dyke*, a 1000 ft. trap dyke to the left of the buttress (D.) is recommended.

Bealach Mhic Coinnich (2928 ft.), see also Coireachan Ruadha. [4]

To gain this col on the Lagan side requires scrambling. One must first ascend the Alaisdair Stone Shoot. It is straightforward on the Coruisk side.

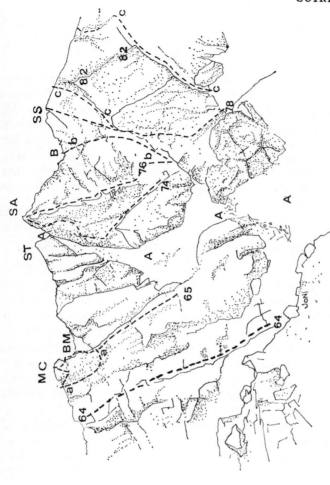

Fig. 7. Upper Coire Lagan from Sgurr Dearg

A   Alasdair stone-shoot
B   Pass to Coire d'Ghrunnda
BM Bealach MhicCoinnich
MC Sgurr MhicCoinnich
SA Sgurr Alasdair
SS Sgurr Sgumain
ST Sgurr Thearlaich

a–a easy route from Bealach
     MhicCoinnich to summit
b–b easy stone-shoot
c–c easy ways to Sgumain
64   Jeffries Dyke
65   West Buttress
74   Abraham's Climb
76   Collie's Climb
78   N. Ridge   82   Prometheus

Sgurr Thearlaich (3208 ft. Charles' Peak – after Charles Pilkington), see also Coireachan Ruadha and Coire a' Ghrunnda and Alaisdair Stone Shoot (below). [4, 12]

The simplest if most tedious ascent is by the Alaisdair Stone Shoot from the top of which a short moderate scramble leads to the summit.

Less arduous is to make the scramble up to the Bealach Mhic Coinnich, then along the south ridge. There is an awkward move just above the col. The west face overlooking the Alaisdair Stone Shoot is steep and seamed with five gullies, all of which were climbed by the early climbers. Of the ribs between the buttresses, only that to the left of the lower (A.) Gully, has provided a worthwhile route (*Lower Rib* 300 ft. S.).

Alaisdair Stone Shoot (see also Coire a' Ghrunnda 4).

The famous scree gully between Sgurr Alaisdair and Mhic Coinnich/Thearlaich was once the longest scree run in the British Isles. Given the energy, the stability, and the boots, one could drop 1500 ft. in less than 10 minutes. Alas no more. Generations of scree-hurtlers have spun down the top layer of small chips, so that today the upper half of the scree is no more than a bed of middle-sized angular rocks which are painful to descend. Nevertheless it still represents a quick and easy way down from the most rugged and highest point in the Cuillin. To the walker seeking this summit it provides an easy if arduous means of ascent.

From the lochan ascend directly towards Sgurr Alaisdair. The scree slope narrows to a point where one must scramble over a few boulders and then fans out again. Trend leftwards towards the Bealach Mhic Coinnich (A-A, Fig. 7) till the walls close in and there is no choice of route.

The length (1200 ft.) and steepness of the stone shoot make it a dangerous place when other parties are about, and though the ascending climber is unlikely to dislodge a stone now, for the track is well beaten out, a descending party can easily do so. If there are people above, one should be very much on the alert for falling rocks.

On its northern or Ghrunnda side the top of the stone shoot which is the col (3020 ft.) between Alaisdair and Thearlaich is deceptive. A gentle scree leads down for 300 ft. then vanishes over a vertical cliff. Beware!

33. Sgurr Alasdair (left) and Sgurr Sgumain (centre). The right skyline ridge of Sgumain is the west buttress. The climb starts at the extreme bottom right. The rake from Coire Lagan is seen. Immediately right of this west ridge is Bealach Coire a'Ghrunnda.

34. Coire Lagan from Sgurr Dearg. From left to right: Alasdair stoneshoot (light mark on scree), Sgurr Alasdair, Sgurr Sgumain, Sron na Ciche.

35. The great north-west face of Sron na Ciche. The Cioch and Cioch Buttress are visible in the centre. The buttress to the left (apparently contiguous, though not so) is Eastern Buttress, and to the right, Western Buttress.

36.   The Cioch from the upper buttress.

Sgurr Alaisdair (3257 ft. Peak of Alexander), see also Coire a' Ghrunnda. [12]

The highest peak in the Cuillin, it was also one of the first ascended, doubtless on account of two things: its magnificent appearance seen from Coire Lagan, from where it so obviously looks the king of mountains, and the fact that the stone-shoot provides a non-technical approach almost to the summit. The ascent was made in 1873 by the then Sheriff of Skye, Alexander Nicholson, after whom the peak is now named.

Appropriately the summit is the finest situation in the Cuillin, indeed in Skye; if not in all Scotland. Its walls fall steeply and the summit is angular and confined, imparting that airiness demanded of all true peaks. Even the easiest ascent calls for 100 ft. of moderate rock climbing. In still weather the lochan in Coire Lagan appears as a zircon pool thousands of feet below. Every Cuillin peak is visible, and an uncountable number of mainland peaks from Ben More in Mull, through Nevis to Beinn Alligin. Westward, beyond the huge sea cliffs, the outer isles squat on the sea like a convoy of ships. And perhaps best of all, with the knowledge of the stone shoot and a rapid descent to terra firma, the climber can confidently linger on the top and watch the sunset.

The 'tourist route', then, is to ascend the stone shoot to the col, and then turn back westwards up the clean rock to the summit, heavily marked and as easy to follow as tracks in the snow.

Another route of simplicity is to trend right after the narrows in the stone shoot and aim for the right hand end of the crags that fall from Alaisdair [b-b, Fig. 7]. Beyond the base of these rocks there are outcrops which are avoided. The col between Sgumain and Alaisdair is reached. The ascent of the S.W. ridge is interesting and has one technical move about V.D., known as the 'Bad Step'. The easiest line lies on the Ghrunnda side, but if this side is held too long, the route becomes more continually difficult, and the trick is to gain the ridge by the technically difficult move to the left at just the right point about 100 ft. from the col. The rocks are all worn, and the trail shows.

For all its magnificence, the west face, when one actually gets onto it, is a good deal less steep than it appears. There are two delightful long routes: *Collie's Climb* (D. 800 ft.), done in 1896, starts to the right of the lowest rocks directly below the Alaisdair-Sgumain col, and holds more or less to the right hand side of the west buttress of Alaisdair. Except on the lower section the rock is excellent and the holds magnificent.

Abraham's Climb (D.) is a more continuous route, and better than Collie's. It starts a little lower and to the left, at the lowest possible point of the crag at a chimney at the end of the final short wall.

The route follows the left edge of a shallow gully running obliquely to the left. An easier stretch leads to the crest of a wall overlooking the Alaisdair Stone shoot. Difficult rocks lead to a projection in the face capable of holding three men. The route trends left to avoid a bulge, and then takes the line of least resistance to the summit. Though an easy climb it has not been unknown for a strong party new to Cuillin to lose themselves on this route in mist.

Sgurr Sgumain (3108 ft. The Stack Peak), see also Coire a' Ghrunnda. [12]

Somewhat eclipsed by its neighbour when seen from afar, this peak shows itself to great advantage when seen from Lochan Coire Lagan. To the right of the stone shoot between Alaisdair and Sgumain is the *North Buttress* (M.), a long route without problems climbed by Pilkington's party in 1887 [78, Fig. 7]. Half way up a scree shoot trends to the right, and leads without meeting further rocks to the crest below the final tower of the West Buttress. The west flank holds several fine hard routes, such as the *Direct Route*, N. Buttress (600 ft. V.S.). Other easy routes are shown (c-c) on Fig. 7.

The west spur of Sgumain is a fine ridge, offering 1600 ft. of climbing – the *West Buttress* (D.). There is much choice of route. The shattered rock of summit arête the *West Buttress* (D.) is usually turned by a small chimney some distance to the right. It is on the flanks of this ridge that many new climbs on excellent rock have been made. As one approaches Coire Lagan a slanting rake will be observed to ascend from left to right from the floor of Coire Lagan to the plateau of Sron na Ciche. This rake cuts through the lower portion of the west ridge, vanishes into the Sgumain stone shoot that falls from the col between Sgumain and Sron na Ciche, and continues across the face of Sron na Ciche. At the Lagan end the rake is indicated by cairns (a-a, Fig. 8.) and is a useful access route from upper Coire Lagan to the upper portions of Sron na Ciche. *Sunset Slab* (600 ft. V.D.) starts at the prominent white blaze above the rake.

The *West Trap* route by those two mountain explorers, J. H. Bell and F.S. Smythe, was the earliest (1924), and follows this conspicuous trap dyke.

Bealach Coire a' Ghrunnda

This col lies at the head of the Sgumain Stone Shoot, that lies between the West Buttress of Sgumain and Eastern Buttress of Sron na Ciche. From it one almost traverses into Coire a' Ghrunnda. It is without difficulty on both sides. B.G., Fig. 8.

Sron na Ciche (approx. 2500 ft. Spur of the Cioch), see also Coire a' Ghrunnda. [12]

This is less a peak than a spur of Sgumain. It nevertheless dominates the west end of Coire Lagan because its N.W. wall is the greatest cliff in the Cuillin, almost half a mile long and a thousand feet high. It is made famous by the remarkable rock projection so aptly named by the earthy ancients as the Cioch or breast. It consists largely of rough gabbro intersected with basaltic dykes, which decomposing more easily than gabbro, form gullies and chimneys. Its accessibility from Glen Brittle and the excellence of the rock has resulted in an almost 'Welsh' level of route proliferation. This is the Cuillin playground. Those who wish their mountains to themselves had better not come to this face in high summer.

The face is bounded to the right or west by the flank of the mountain which rises as a steep hillside from the moor below. To the left is the Sgumain Stone Shoot. The face is divided into three sections by Eastern Gully and Central Gully. (Fig. 8).

The easiest route to Sron na Ciche summit is by the west flank. This is a pleasant descent after the final climb of the day. The Sgumain Stone Shoot, dropping from the barely noticeable col, Bealach a' Coir' Ghrunnda, is another easy route, used mostly on descent.

The three divisions will be described from left to right.

EASTERN BUTTRESS

Eastern Buttress lies between the Sgumain Stone Shoot and Eastern Gully. The stone shoot is an easy scree run. *Eastern Gully* is severe, and was climbed in 1913 by Steeple and Barlow. There are two pitches at the foot, both usually wet. The second pitch can be

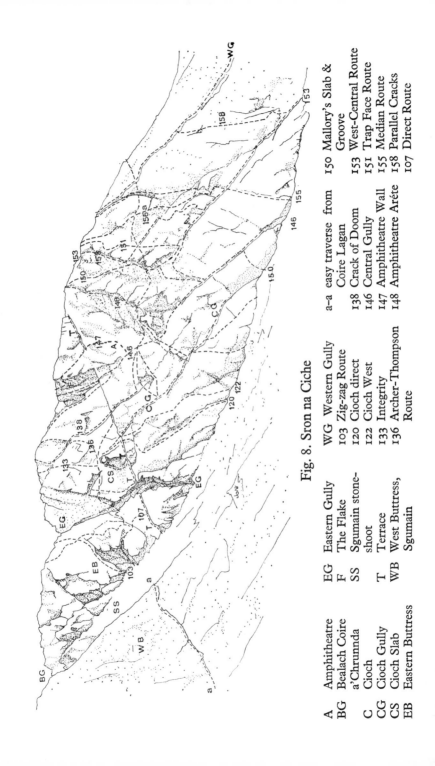

Fig. 8. Sron na Ciche

A	Amphitheatre	EG	Eastern Gully	WG Western Gully
BG	Bealach Coire a'Chrunnda	F	The Flake	103 Zig-zag Route
		SS	Sgumain stone-shoot	120 Cioch direct
C	Cioch			122 Cioch West
CG	Cioch Gully	T	Terrace	133 Integrity
CS	Cioch Slab	WB	West Buttress, Sgumain	136 Archer-Thompson Route
EB	Eastern Buttress			

a-a	easy traverse from Coire Lagan	150 Mallory's Slab & Groove
138	Crack of Doom	153 West-Central Route
146	Central Gully	151 Trap Face Route
147	Amphitheatre Wall	155 Median Route
148	Amphitheatre Aréte	158 Parallel Cracks
		107 Direct Route

avoided by the ascent of a crack to the left, followed by a delicate traverse, which forms part of the Sron na Ciche girdle traverse. Though Collie, with his gift for the easiest line, found *Zigzag* (m.103) in 1912, and Steeple, Barlow, and Doughty did the exhilarating direct route of 600 ft. (V.D., 107) in 1912, the main development of interesting routes has all been post war. *Vulcan Wall* was the name given by McInnes to the prominent high wall on the east face (left) of the buttress. Originally done with artificial aids, it is now a free climb starting at the left hand corner of the wall.

Perhaps the most interesting route, and certainly the longest is the *Snake*, climbed by Sproul, Renny and Hall in 1965. It follows a very obvious trap line up the face. There are many routes on the Cioch face of the buttress. *Shangri La* (S.) by Clough and Nicholls is an excellent sustained route.

CIOCH BUTTRESS

Bounded by Eastern Gully and Cioch Gully (itself to the left of Central Gully), this buttress provides some of the finest climbing and situations to be found anywhere on a mountain.

The slanting rake already alluded to divides the rock wall into distinct areas. Above it a smooth 200-ft. sweep of slabs provides a perfect setting for the obtruding *Cioch*, which cast a great shadow across in the slabs in the afternoon sun.

Below the rake and to the right of *Eastern Gully* is a small shallow gully leading up only as far as the rake. It is known as *Little Gully*. The finest route to the rake is unquestionably *Cioch Direct*, [120] the 1907 climb of A. P. Abraham and H. Harland, a 500-ft. severe with some superb situations. It starts to the right of *Little Gully* about 300 ft. above the lowest point of the screes, and follows a crack line right up the face. The topmost chimney is the crux. Several parallel lines have been made to right and left of the Cioch Direct, many of them harder. McNaught–Davis *Cioch Grooves* (V.S.) is superb.

A climb of great popularity with some fine situations, including a dramatic (but not difficult) traverse is the *Cioch West* route (V.D. 122). Starting to the right of the low point of the buttress it ascends a prominent chimney and continues the line for 300 ft. A well-worn grass ledge leads to an 80 ft. wall, followed by a sensational traverse to the left. The climb gains the terrace or rake below the Cioch at the right hand end, so that a satisfying continuation is feasible by one of the many routes up the Cioch, such as the *Cioch Nose*, which though only Difficult, is a superbly airy route.

The simplest route up the Cioch is to ascend *Little* or *Eastern Gully*, and traverse right till one is under the Cioch Slabs. Collie's route (M.) holds to the deep cracks to the left of the slabs that enter into Eastern Gully higher up. Enter the gully for 50 ft., and then traverse back to the Cioch neck on a ledge below the Cioch buttress. A popular route, is the highly polished *Slab Corner* (D.) which also leads to the neck, but is not advised in moist weather.

From the neck a short move lands one on the slab top of the Cioch. It is a vantage point that is aesthetically and technically satisfying. The great routes of the upper buttress may be easily picked out, for one is cantilevered out from the face. Seawards the composition of ocean and islands is delectably framed by the shoulder of Sron na Ciche. Groundwards there is little interruption till the scree 600 ft. below.

Cioch Gully is another route to the Cioch which has its charm, and gets harder (V.D.) as one ascends. Since stones from the upper climbs may fall this way, the climb is not recommended when climbers are on the upper buttress.

The upper buttress of the Cioch provides some of the best climbing in the British Isles. It is not necessary to ascend the Cioch to reach this point. One can traverse in from high on Eastern Gully. Contrary to appearances there are quite simple routes up the forbidding steepness of the upper buttress. The traditional easy way is *Archer-Thomson's* route (D., 136) which holds up a steep groove never as hard as it looks. It starts from the right of the grass patch behind the Cioch. Here too starts one of the hardest and best routes in Skye, Walsh and McKay's *Trophy Crack* (V.S.). A large flake forms a prominent crack and overhangs.

Left of this is *Integrity* (S., 133) which is a fine route on superb rock. Further left again one of the first truly artificial routes, McInnes and Clough's *Atropos* (V.S.: A.3).

But it is to Pye and Shadbolt's remarkable *Crack of Doom* (S., 138) that some of the finest situations on the upper face must go. This curving crack is very conspicuous even from the corrie. Yet right again is the logical next step – *The Crack of Double Doom* by Haworth and Hughes. An easy fault leads to the apex of a slab. The crux demands some caution on jammed rocks that don't look as if they are destined to remain there forever.

THE WESTERN BUTTRESS OF SRON NA CICHE

The western buttress is bounded by the right hand end of the crag and Central Gully. It is almost impossible to make out features when on the wall, but they stand out well enough when walking up the corrie below, several rakes slant up the face. The Cioch terrace rake passes Central Gully below a prominent mass of rock that reaches to the skyline – The Flake. Immediately below the terrace and to the right is the Amphitheatre whose prominent right wall is Amphitheatre arête, up which Collie found a Moderate route in 1907. It is possible to gain this route from the floor of the corrie. To the right is a deep depression followed by another arête. This one is the much more challenging West Central arête up which runs the Trap Face route (1000 ft. V.S.). Between here and the western margin of the face is the western buttress proper, which is not so hard as it looks. The whole face is complex and large, and it is hard both to describe and to follow routes. Variations are common.

Three routes will be mentioned as worthy of attention.

Mallory's Slab and Groove (1000 ft. S., 150).

The start of this route is midway between Central and Cioch Gullies at a prominent crack immediately to the right of an overhang. The crack is climbed to gain Central Gully, which is followed for 150 ft. till another prominent crack on the right leads one out onto the face and onto the wall to the right of Amphitheatre arête.

Amphitheatre Wall (600 ft. V.S., 147) is one of the best Skye V.S. climbs. The wall lies at the back of the Amphitheatre above the great slabs, which can be reached in a variety of ways, for example up Central Gully, the lower section of which is easy. Alternatively one may ascend by *Amphitheatre arête* (M. 148). Several routes have been put up on this wall and share pitches. Even the easiest line is of considerable severity and very sustained.

COIR A' GHRUNNDA

(1)	**Sron na Ciche**	2500 ft. approx.
(2)	**Sgurr Sgumain**	3108 ft.
(3)	**Sgurr Alaisdair**	3257 ft.
(4)	**Sgurr Thearlaich**	3208 ft.
(5)	**Sgurr Dubh na da Bheinn**	3078 ft.
(6)	**Sgurr nan Eag**	3031 ft.

This corrie bears the unmistakable stamp of the ice age. The terminal moraine is obvious, while the slabs of the lower corrie are ice-scarred. The corrie is in two tiers, with rock climbs on both, but is nowhere so hemmed in with crags as is Coire Lagan. Loch Coir' a' Ghrunnda at 2300 ft. provides an exquisite foreground to the view southwards out of the corrie, and is the highest sheet of water in Skye, and remarkably close to the main ridge 320 ft. above.

The path from Glen Brittle takes a lower line than that to Coire Lagan, and leaves that path below Loch an Fhir-bhallaich. It skirts the lower slopes of Sron na Ciche, and then once in the corrie, holds well to the left. Once in the corrie the way is cairned. In mist one need only remember to keep to the west of the issuing burn. One may cross back to Glen Brittle by the Bealach Coir' Ghrunnda and to Coir' Uisg by the Bealach Garbh Coire.

Sron na Ciche, see also Coire Lagan. [11]

As one turns into the corrie the left or west wall is revealed as broad crag, divided into the South (the lower) and the North crag. The South is steep and slabby, and provides the better climbing of the two. Its most prominent feature is a large whitish slab high up on its face, which gives its name to the most popular route, the *White Slab Route* (600 ft. V.D. 165). A gully divides the face and the route lies on the rock to the left, the direct route (S.) taking a more direct line and closer to the gully in the lower section. See Fig. 9

The North crag stands to the north, higher up the corrie, and separated from the lower crag by open rocks and a water-course. It is

37.   Sgurr Alasdair and Sgurr Sgumain from the south (Sgurr nan Eag).

38. Lochan Coire a'Ghrunnda from Sgurr nan Eag. The two peaks at the head of the screes are Sgurr Alasdair (left) and Sgurr Thearlaich. Sgurr Sgumain, here insignificant, stands to the left and seen through the col between them is the Inaccessible Pinnacle of Sgurr Dearg.

39. The steep Ghrunnda face crags of Sgurr Thearlaich (left), cut by the notch of the Thearlaich-Dubh gap. The peak to the right is Sgurr Dubh Mor, the col between being the Bealach Coire an Lochan.

41. McLeod's Maidens, Idrigill Point.

40. Opposite: View across Loch Brittle to the Coire Lagan group of peaks, with Sgurr Alasdair prominent.

42. Kilt Rock, Staffin.

43.   Neist Point.

44. Dunvegan Castle.

divided by a gully into two buttresses offering Moderate and Difficult routes.

To gain the upper corrie and lochan one must climb above the base of the North crag. At the Loch a short walk up scree leads to the scarcely defined saddle between Sron na Ciche and Sgumain, called Bealach Coir' a' Ghrunnda, and which leads down to the Sgumain Stone shoot.

Sgurr Sgumain (3108 ft.), see also Coire Lagan. [II]

This mountain has no character seen from this side, offering simply a scree slope.

Sgurr Alaisdair (3257 ft.), and Sgurr Thearlaich. See also Coire Lagan. [11]

The south face of Alaisdair falls into the corrie, and forms a continuous wall with the south face of Sgurr Sgumain. The only easy route to Alaisdair is to the Sgumain-Alaisdair col (which can be gained from this side or the Coire Lagan side) and up the west ridge (see Coire Lagan). All other routes require a high standard of rock climbing, though the next easiest is to gain the Thearlaich-Dubh gap, and ascend via the south ridge of Sgurr Thearlaich. The base of the cliffs is a little below the level of the Sgumain-Alaisdair col. They may be reached by traversing from that col or from the Bealach à Garbh Choire. All the climbs finish near the summits.

The west part of the face, left of the Alaisdair summit is broken. The first climb coming from the left is *West Gully* (V.D.) climbed by Steeple, Barlow, and Doughty. After 200 ft. it opens out on to the face. 60 yards to its right, and 70 yards from the Thearlaich-Dubh gap a prominent crack rises from a cave. This is *Commando Crack* and gives an excellent Severe climb. Two diedres are to be found here. *Con's Cleft* (V.S.) starts about 100 ft. to the left of the Gap, while McInnes' *Grand Dièdre* (V.S.) on the buttress on the north side of the Gap.

Sgurr Dubh na da Bheinn (3078 ft.), see also An Garbh Choire. [2]

This peak is a walk up the scree from the Loch either direct or via the cols to each side. The west side is broken into small crags which offer no difficulty on the ascent.

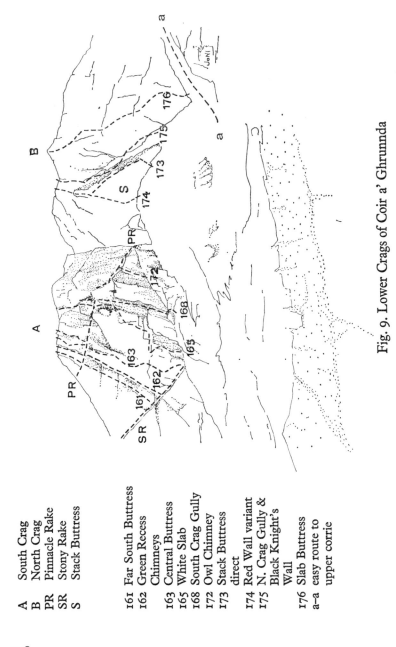

Fig. 9. Lower Crags of Coir a' Ghrunnda

A   South Crag
B   North Crag
PR Pinnacle Rake
SR Stony Rake
S   Stack Buttress

161 Far South Buttress
162 Green Recess
    Chimneys
163 Central Buttress
165 White Slab
168 South Crag Gully
172 Owl Chimney
173 Stack Buttress
    direct
174 Red Wall variant
175 N. Crag Gully &
    Black Knight's
    Wall
176 Slab Buttress
a–a easy route to
    upper corrie

Sgurr na Eag (3031 ft.), see also An Garbh Choire. [2]

The traverse of this peak is without difficulty. A buttress of some size falls on the west side in the corrie just opposite the South Crag of Sron na Ciche. Though broken, it contains a prominent curving crack that offers a 600 ft. of Difficult climbing with many escapes, leading almost to the summit.

SECTION 13

COIRE AN LAOIGH

(1)	**Sgurr na Eag**	3031 ft.
(2)	**Sgurr a' Choire Bhig**	2872 ft.
(3)	**Garsbheinn**	2935 ft.

This, the Calf's corrie, is the most open and least spectacular of the Cuillin. However, it faces to the southern ocean, and the prospect is delightful.

It is a walk of some three hours from Glen Brittle to gain the corrie, and once there the peaks at either side may be easily climbed by their west ridges. Within the corrie is a 500 ft. high band of slabs, cut by two prominent gullies. The slabs provide severe climbing. The *West Gully* is Moderate, the *Central Gully* V.D.

For descriptions and details of the summits see An Garbh Choire.

CUILLIN RIDGE

The traverse of the Cuillin main ridge is the finest mountain excursion in the British Isles. From sea level back to sea level involves an ascent of some 10,000 ft. To do this in one day therefore involves a degree of fitness. To do it without a fair knowledge of the ridge would be almost impossible, for the delays occasioned by route-finding, not to mention the loss of impetus, would sap any party. Of course, many parties elect to do the ridge in two or more days, carrying bivouac gear, or arranging depots. But for those who have done it the traverse of the ridge in one day remains as one of life's most satisfying mountaineering experiences, Alps and far flung ranges notwithstanding.

The first traverse was effected by L. G. Shadbolt and A. C. McLaren on June 10, 1911, in 12 hours and 20 minutes, Garsbheinn to Gillean. Their timetable was as follows:

Leave	Glen Brittle	03.35	
Arrive	Garsbheinn	06.05	
	Sgurr nan Eag	06.50	
	Sgurr Dubh na da Bheinn	07.45	(25 minute halt)
	Sgurr Alaisdair	09.00	
	Sgurr Mhic Coinnich	09.50	
	Inaccessible Pinnacle	10.55	(45 minute halt on Sgurr Dearg)
	Sgurr a' Ghreadaidh	13.07	
	Bidein Druim nan Ramh	14.40	(40 minute halt)
	Bruach na Frithe	16.45	
	Sgurr nan Gillean	18.25	(30 minute rest at Bealach na Lice)
	Sligachan	20.20	

In 1914 Howard Somervell made the solo traverse, summit to summit in 10½ hours, which today is considered fair time for a competent party. In 1932 Bicknell recorded a time of 8 hours, also on a solo expedition. The fastest time ever claimed was that done by Eric Beard, in 1966. He took 4 hours 9 minutes from Garsbheinn to Sgurr nan Gillean. It is clear that the solo climber makes the best time. Generally he will want to carry a rope to assist him on the Thearlaich-Dubh gap. A party is bound to move slower, but has the advantage that the rope weight can be shared, and there are fewer risks to run. The principal problem is nearly always water, and even though water may be found not far from the ridge at the Bealach na Lice in the Fionn Choire, the thought of an extra few hundred feet of climbing generally oppresses all but the thirstiest or hardiest. As an example of the problems, the author of this guide when doing the traverse left Garsbheinn with four pints of water and six oranges, yet cringingly borrowed a slug of water from a South African party found bivouacked on the col between Caisteal and Druim nan Ramh.

Since total energy is a factor in the traverse, the starting and finishing point have great relevance. It is common practice to start at Glen Brittle, head for Garsbheinn, and traverse to Sligachan, where one either buys a bed, or has one's friends waiting. More elegant in that it imparts better sense of completeness is to start and finish at Coruisk. Garsbheinn lies directly above the hut, and at the day's end, one can take in Sgurr nan Uamh without significant deviation, drop into Harta Corrie, climb slightly over the flanks of Druim nan Ramh to Loch a' Choire Riabhach, and regain one's starting point. Garsbheinn from Coruisk takes less than 2 hours, and from Sgurr nan Uamh to Coruisk is a 2½-hour tramp. A start from Coruisk also has the merit that if the traverse is abandoned for any reason, base is always near at hand.

GREATER CUILLIN TRAVERSE

The traverse is held to include Clach Glas and Blaven. This incredible feat, involving 13,500 ft. of climbing, was achieved by I. G. Charleson and W. E. Forde in June 1939. They took about 18 hours. However, the ultimate, the traverse of all the Black Cuillin peaks in one day has yet to be accomplished. This would include outriders like An Diollaid, Sgurr a' Bhasteir, Garbh Bheinn and Sgurr nan Eag and Belig.

WINTER TRAVERSE

Winter being a fickle thing in the island of Skye, the conditions for a true winter traverse do not occur often. The first successful attempt was made on January 31 and February 1, 1965. The shortage of daylight will almost certainly preclude this feat being compressed into one day. The first winter traverse was done by T. W. Patey, B. Robertson, H. McInnes, and D. Crabbe. They gained Gillean by the col with the fourth pinnacle, and found the West Ridge grade III. Above 2000 ft. the snow was hard and excellent for cramponning. They bivouacked on Sgurr na Banachdich, having had appropriate gear ferried up to them from Glen Brittle by helpers. The Inaccessible Pinnacle was grade IV, as was the Thearlaich-Dubh gap. Several photos of that historic traverse are in this guide (photo 37, 31, 29, 19).

WINTER CLIMBING

It has been calculated that no part of the Island of Skye is more than five miles from the sea. Moreover the western sea is warmed by the gulf stream. In such circumstances frost rarely gets a grip, and whole winters may pass without appreciable snowfall on the Cuillin. See the section on weather in Introduction.

The Cuillins respond as magnificently as any range to snow cover. Even the spurned scree heaps of Glamaig or Sgurr a' Bhasteir assume supernatural stature. And it may happen anytime from October to May. The trouble is that snow rarely lasts. Deep snow or frost all come rarely. Frost is the commoner, linked with seemingly perpetual anti-cyclones in which the brown winter landscape is tinged in golden light, and even the merest hummock throws its long slender pinnacle of shadow over the moor. It can snow a foot or more, and be gone in 24 hours, licked away by a warm south-wester. Yet, the twin conditions of snowfall and frost do come, as they did recently in 1962 and 1965. In April 1962 Sgurr Alaisdair's summit mass stuck out of the compacted nevé of Coire à Ghrunnda like a Dolomite peak. In January 1965 coherent snow was well established and permitted the first winter traverse.

The Cuillin winter is a chance. A phone call will save a lot of useless journeying. But the experience is worth having. Rarely will there be the consolation to be found annually on the mainland precipices like Meagaidh and Nevis, but almost every winter there will be moments of magnificence. And, of course, the high latitude, the low light, the clarity of the air make any sunny winter's day a superb experience, snow or not. It is well to remember that the days are short and the risks are long.

See 'winter traverse', section 14.

45. Macrimmon's Cairn – Boreraig, looking south.

46.   Dunvegan from the west, looking over the sea loch.

47.   Below: Glendale, looking west towards the hills of Waterstein Head.

48. The road into Glendale and Loch Pooltiel in Duirinish.

PEAKS AND PASSES OF THE CUILLIN

Many of the heights of peaks given in the earlier editions of the Ordnance Survey have been found to be incorrect, and in this Guide the latest values are given (1969). (T.S.) for trigonometrical stations.

The heights of bealachs and of a few minor peaks are based chiefly on aneroid readings made by members of the S.M.C. They are marked 'ap'. Heights given are in feet. The number after a corrie indicates the section in the text.

THE MAIN GROUP

Sgurr nan Gillean, 3167 (T.S.) = the peak of the young men, or (Norse) the peak of ghylls, lies 3 m. S.S.W. of Sligachan Hotel.

(*a*) From the summit a branch ridge runs N.N.E., dividing Coire a' Bhasteir on the W. from Glen Sligachan on the E. This is the Pinnacle Ridge. The fourth pinnacle, or Knight's Peak, lying next to Sgurr nan Gillean, is 2994. The third is 2892; the second, 2650; and the first, 2500 ap.

(*b*) From the summit a branch ridge runs S.E., dividing Lota Corrie on the W. from Coire nan Allt Geala on the E. It ends in **Sgurr na h-Uamha,** 2416, pron. *Sgurr na Hoo-a* = the peak of the cave, which lies 1 m. S. by E. from Sgurr nan Gillean. The lowest point on this ridge is 2099. A small peak lies between this and Sgurr nan Gillean, ½ m. S.E. by S. from the latter, and is called on the 6-inch map **Sgurr Beag,** 2530 ap. This is the ridge by which the tourist makes the ascent. He joins it between the summit and Sgurr Beag at a height of 2360 ap.

From the summit the main ridge runs westward to the Tooth of Sgurr nan Gillean and

7 Coire a' Bhasteir (executioner's corrie).	BEALACH A' BHASTEIR, 2733 (an easy pass).	Lota Corrie (loft corrie). **6**

Am Bhasteir, 3069 = the executioner (probably in reference to the outline of the Bhasteir Tooth, which may be thought to resemble a headsman's axe), ½ m. W. of Sgurr nan Gillean.

Bhasteir Tooth, 3005, lies immediately under Am Basteir to the W.

(*a*) From 50 yards W. of the Tooth a branch ridge runs N. for ¼ m., with a dip at 2865 ap., and ending in **Sgurr a' Bhasteir,** 2951. It separates Fionn Choire from Coire a' Bhasteir.

7	Fionn Choire (fair corrie).	BEALACH NAN LICE, 2940 ap., pron. *Leeka* = pass of the flat stones (an easy pass, This was formerly called BEALACH A' LEITIR.	Lota Corrie.	6

Sgurr a' Fionn Choire, 3068, a small peak immediately W. of the pass.

7	Fionn Choire.	Dip, 2964 ap.	Lota Corrie.	6

Bruach na Frithe, 3143 (T.S.), pron. *Bruach na Free* = the brae of the forest, ¾ m. W. of Sgurr nan Gillean.

(*a*) From the summit a branch ridge runs N.W. to Sron an Tobar nan Uaislean, 1682, and Bealach a' Mhaim, 1132.

From the summit of Bruach na Frithe the main ridge turns to the S., running without any well-marked break to

8	Coir' a' Tarneilear (foxes corrie).	Dip, 2772	Lota Corrie.	6

Sgurr na Bhairnich, 2826 = the limpet, lies ½ m. S. of the summit of Bruach na Frithe.

8	Coir' a' Tarneilear.	Dip, 2520 ap. This deeply cut cleft is one of the lowest points of the main ridge. Descent into Tarneilear by a stone shoot. From the gully on the E. side it is possible to reach Lota Corrie by a short rock wall just above where the gully takes a great plunge down the lower precipices.	Harta Corrie.	6

An Caisteal, 2724 = the castle.

	Coir' a' Tarneilear	BEALACH, 2494 (an easy pass).	Harta Corrie.

North Peak, Bidein Druim nan Ramh, 2794, pron. *Bidyin Drim na Raav* = the peaks of the ridge of oars, lies ¾ m. S.S.W. of Bruach na Frithe.

8	Coir' a' Tarneilear	Gap, 2700 ap.	Harta Corrie.	6

Central Peak, Bidein Druimn an Ramh, 2850, lies about 70 yards S.S.W. of the North Peak.

(*a*) From the Central Peak a branch ridge called **Druim nan Ramh** runs S.E. for 2½ m., dividing Harta Corrie from Coruisk. Before terminating this ridge sends off an eastward extension to the parallel ridge of **Druim Hain** and **Sgurr Hain,** and thence S.W. to the isolated **Sgurr na Stri,** 1623 = peak of strife, overlooking Loch Scavaig.

| 8 | Coir' a' Tarneilear | Gap, with natural bridge, 2710 ap. (an easy scree gully for descent into Coir' a' Tarneilear.) | Glac Mhor and Coruisk (water cauldron). | 5 |

West Peak, Bidein Druim nan Ramh, 2779, lies about 60 yards W. by N. of the Central Peak.

(*a*) From the West Peak a branch ridge runs for ½ m. N.W. towards Coire na Creiche (the corrie of the spoil, so called from a battle having been fought there in 1601 between the Macdonalds and the Macleods) and ends with **Sgurr an Fheadain,** 2215 ap., Pron. *Sgurr an Aityan* = peak of the water-pipe. This ridge divides Coir' a' Mhadaidh on the N.E. from Tairneilear on the S.W.

From the West Peak the main ridge runs nearly W. to

| 8 | Coir' a' Mhadaidh | BEALACH NA GLAIC MOIRE, 2492 ap. = pass of the big hollow | Glac Mhor and Coruisk. | 5 |

North-East Peak, Sgurr, a' Mhadaidh, 2939, pron. *Sgurr a Vatee* = the foxes' peak, 1 m. S.W. from Bruach na Frithe.

| 8 | Mhadaidh | Dip, 2858. | Coire an Uaigneis (corrie of solitude) and Coruisk. | 5 |

Second Peak, Sgurr a' Mhadaidh, 2910.

| 8 | Mhadaidh | Dip, 2840. | Coire an Uaigneis. | 5 |

Third Peak, Sgurr a' Mhadaidh, 2934

| 8 | Mhadaidh | Dip, 2820. (Descent into Coire an Uaigneis by an easy rake.) | Coire an Uaigneis. | 5 |

The ridge is here complicated by sheets of gabbro cutting it obliquely.

After passing a small pinnacle and a gap 20 ft. deep the direction of the ridge turns abruptly S. to

South-West Peak, Sgurr a' Mhadaidh, 3012

This peak has a summit ridge running S. from a point 2970 ap., near the above-mentioned pinnacle, to the highest point 3010 (cairn), without dipping more than 5 ft. The top is a narrow crest-line connecting the cairned point with another point of equal height 30 ft. beyond.

(a) From the northern end of the summit ridge, a shattered ridge dividing Coire a' Mhadaidh from Coire na Dorus runs W.N.W. to **Sgurr Thuilm,** 2885 (T.S.), pron. *Hulim* = peak of Tulm, with a bealach at 2452 ap. The main ridge continues S. to

9 Coire na Dorus (corrie of the door), the N.E. branch of Coire a' Ghreadaidh.

AN DORUS, 2779 = the door. (This is marked An Dorus on the O.S. map.) The descent into Coire na Dorus is easy. On the Coruisk side there is a narrow gully with several small pitches.

Coire an Uaigneis. **5**

From this pass the ridge rising to Sgurr a' Ghreadaidh is interrupted by a narrow gap now known as EAG DUBH, 2890 ap. = black notch. An easy scree gully leads into Coire na Dorus, but the only approach on the Coruisk side is by a difficult gully, and it is therefore no longer possible to regard this as the Macleod's Gap, a pass said to be used by the Macleods and called An Dorus.

North Top, Sgurr a' Ghreadaidh, 3192, pron. *Sgurr Greeta* = the peak

of the 'thrashings' or 'mighty winds' (or in Icelandic, 'the peak of the clear waters'), lies ½ m. S. of the S.W. peak of Sgurr a' Mhadaidh. Sgurr a' Ghreadaidh has a long narrow crest-line with two summits, besides a wart-like prominence just N. of the chief summit.

(a) In a direction N.W. from this prominence, but starting about 200 ft. down on the western face, a spur runs off to a point at about 2700 ap. This is named **Sgurr Eadar da Choire** = the peak between the corries.

Dip between the tops, 3133.

South Top, Sgurr a' Ghreadaidh, 3181

(a) From the summit of the south top a short branch ridge runs E.S.E., dividing Coire an Uaigneis from Coireachan Ruadha.

| 9 | Coire a' Ghreadaidh, south branch. | Dip, 2780. Not a pass, but descent into Coire a' Ghreadaidh can be made without much difficulty. | Coireachan Ruadha (red corries) and Coruisk. | 4 |

Three small teeth, 2950 ap.

Dip, 2925 ap.

Sgurr Thormaid, 3040 = Norman's peak (in honour of Professor J. Norman Collie), lies scarcely $\frac{1}{2}$ m. S.W. of Sgurr a' Ghreadaidh. It was formerly called the North Top of Banachdich.

(a) From here a short spur runs into Coire a' Ghreadaidh.

| 9 | Coire a' Ghreadaidh, south branch. | BEALACH, 2914. Descent into Coire a' Ghreadaidh, first a short rough scramble, then easy, turning to right round 'short spur'. Descent into Coireachan Ruadha presents no difficulty except from unstable screes. | Coireachan Ruadha. | 4 |

North Top (highest), Sgurr na Banachdich, 3166 (T.S.) = small-pox peak (possibly on account of a peculiar rock formation in the corrie from which the peak is named). The alternative name, Sgurr na Banachaig = the milkmaid's peak, is also used locally. In the corrie there are remains of old shielings, which had probably been used for cheese-making when the cows were on the upper pastures.

(a) From the summit a long branch ridge, **Sgurr nan Gobhar** = peak of goats, runs off to W., terminating at a cairn 2047 (T.S.). From this ridge, at about 2700, the shorter spur of **An Diallaid** = the saddle, runs off to N.W., with a dip 2365 ap. and summit 2375 ap. There is an easy descent by way of Coir' an Eich = corrie of horses lying between Sgurr nan Gobhar and An Diallaid.

| 10 | Coire na Banachdich. | Dip, 3010 ap. | Coireachan Ruadha. | 4 |

Second Top, Sgurr na Banachdich, 3089.

| 10 | Coire na Banachdich. | Dip, 2979. | Coireachan Ruadha. | 4 |

Third Top, Sgurr na Banachdich, 3023.

| 10 | Coire na Banachdich. | Dip, 2845 (alternative pass). | Coireachan Ruadha. | 4 |

Southern End of Banachdich Range, 2887 ap.

(*a*) From here a spur, **Sron Bhuidhe**, about 2650, runs off to E.N.E., dividing Coireachan Ruadha into two small corries.

10 Coire na Banachdich.	BEALACH COIRE NA BANACHDICH, 2791. This is probably the easiest pass between Glen Brittle and Coruisk.	Coireachan Ruadha.	**4**

Gap just before precipice of Dearg, 2910 ap.

Sgurr Dearg, 3209 (T.S.), pron. *Sgurr jerrack* = the red peak, lies ½ m. S.S.E. of Sgurr na Banachdich.

(*a*) From the cairn of Sgurr Dearg a ridge dividing Coire na Banachdich from Coire Lagan runs S. to a slight dip, then W. to a marked summit 3049, and terminates at the cairn of **Sron Dearg,** 2012. From a point about 2535 on this ridge a short spur called the Window Tower Buttress runs off N.W., with tower at 2190 ap.

Dip, 3180.

Inaccessible Pinnacle, 3234, lies 100 ft. S.S.E. of the cairn.

The main ridge continues in a general S.E. direction to

Dip, 3090 ap.

An Stac, 3125 = the stack.

An easy descent from Sgurr Dearg to Coire Lagan can be made over screes, skirting W. base of Inaccessible Pinnacle and An Stac, and bearing to left till near the bealach. The scree leading more directly towards the corrie runs over a precipice.

11 Coire Lagan (corrie of the hollow).	BEALACH COIRE LAGAN, 2690. Descent into Coireachan Ruadha troublesome for the first. 300 or 400 ft., having rotten rock at top and smooth slabs below; the latter may be avoided by keeping away to the left.	Coireachan Ruadha and Coruisk.	**4**

The gap, 2639, about 120 yards S.E. of bealach is the lowest point, but is not a pass.

Sgurr Mhic Coinnich, 3111 = Mackenzie's peak, lies ½ m. S.E. of Sgurr Dearg.

11 Coire Lagan.	BEALACH MHIC COINNICH, 2928 ap. Descent into Coire Lagan – first a short rock scramble, then a scree gully joining the Alasdair Stone Shoot at about 2500. Descent on other side into Coireachan Ruadha, or on to col of Sgurr Coire an Lochain, presents no difficulty.	Coireachan Ruadha	**4**

Sgurr Thearlaich, 3208 = peak of Charles. This used to be called the N.E. Peak of Alasdair.

(*a*) From the northern end of Sgurr Thearlaich a ridge, at first ill defined, runs N.E. for ½ m., separating Coireachan Ruadha from Coir' an Lochain. After a dip at 2444 the ridge rises to **Sgurr Coire an Lochain,** with highest point 2491, which is divided by a deep gap, 2336, from the north top, 2398.

Leaving the main ridge at Sgurr Thearlaich to traverse the important ridge to the S.W., there is from the summit a steep descent to

11	Coire Lagan.	Dip, 3135. Head of 'Alaisdair Stone Shoot' from Coire Lagan. A severe rock-climb on the Ghrunnda side.	Coir' a' Ghrunnda (the floor corrie).

Sgurr Alasdair, 3257 = peak of Alexander, lies close to and W. of Sgurr Thearlaich. It is the highest peak in Skye.

From the summit a ridge runs S.W. to

11	Coire Lagan.	Dip, 3023. Descent over screes on either side.	Coir' a' Ghrunnda.

Sgurr Sgumain, 3108 (T.S.) = the peak stack, lies 200 yards S.W. of Sgurr Alasdair. From near the summit subsidiary ridges run W. and N.W. into Coire Lagan. To the S.S.W. the principal ridge continues to

11	Coire Lagan.	BEALACH COIR' A' GHRUNNDA, 2759. (A useful pass.)	Coir' a' Ghrunnda.

Beyond this the ridge broadens out into the sloping stony plateau of **Sron na Ciche.**

Returning to Sturr Thearlaich the main ridge runs S.E. to

12	Coir' a' Ghrunnda.	THEARLAICH – DUBH GAP, 2950 ap. Descent of gully to Coir' a' Ghrunnda of moderate difficulty. Other side of Gap apparently hopeless.	Coir' an Lochain	**3**

The S.E. wall of the Gap forms a pinnacle, 2980 ap., from which the ridge drops to

12 Coir' a' Ghrunnda. | BEALACH COIR' AN LOCHAIN, 2806. Descent into Coir' a' Ghrunnda easy. If continuing down the corrie, leave the burn where it turns to the left after first steep descent, and passing just below a rough bit of scree, keep up on W. side of Corrie, thus avoiding glaciated slabs. Descent into Coir' an Lochain rough. There is an easy way to Coruisk from Coir' an Lochain. At the mouth of the corrie, on the right, a cairn marks the top of this way. One may walk straight down a ledge which runs eastwards to Coir' a' Chaoruinn, emerging into this through a small natural arch at about 1200 ft. altitude. | Coir' an Lochain. **3**

Sgurr Dubh na Da Bheinn, 3078, pron. *Sgurr Doo na Da Ven* = the black peak of the two hills (meaning perhaps the peak at the junction of two ridges), lies nearly ½ m. E.S.E. of Sgurr Alasdair.

From this peak a long ridge runs E. to

2 An Garbh-choire (rough corrie)   Dip, 2907.   Coir' an Lochain. **3**

Sgurr Dubh Mor, 3096, pron. *Sgurr Doo Mor* = the big black peak, lies ¼ m. E. of Sgurr Dubh na Da Bheinn. (From the summit a branch ridge runs to the N., separating Coir' an Lochain from Coir' a' Chaoruinn.)

2 An Garbh-choire.   Dip, 2283.   Coir' a' Chaoruinn (rowan corrie).

On the E. side of this dip there is a very steep ascent to

Sgurr Dubh Beag, 2403, pron. *Sgurr Doo Beg* = the little black peak, lies ½ m. E. of Sgurr Dubh Mor.

From the summit the ridge continues eastwards for 1 m. in an unbroken line of slabs to the shore of Loch Coruisk.

Returning to the main ridge, from Sgurr Dubh na Da Bheinn it runs S. to

12 Coir' a' Ghrunnda.   Dip, 2620 ap.   An Garbh-choire. **2**

Caisteal a' Gharbh-choire, 2719 = the castle of the rough corrie, stands at the head of An Garbh-choire.

12	Coir' a' Ghrunnda.	BEALACH A' GHARBH-CHOIRE, 2614 ap. (an easy pass). The direct way down the bottom of An Garbh-choire is made difficult by a chaos of huge blocks of rock; an easier route can be found by keeping to the flank of Sgurr Dubh.	An Garbh-choire.	2

Sgurr nan Eag, 3031 (T.S.) = the notched peak, lies $\frac{1}{2}$ m. S. of Sgurr Dubh na Da Bheinn. It has a nearly level summit ridge running S.E. for 300 or 400 yards: to give it two tops is rather a needless refinement. A broad sloping shoulder extends to the S.W., separating Coir' a' Ghrunnda from Coire nan Laogh.

13	Coire nan Laogh (corrie of the calves).	BEALACH, 2537. To reach Coire nan Laogh easily, either ascend to the shoulder of Sgurr nan Eag or keep up on the slope of Sgurr a' Choire Bhig at first. Descent into An Garbh-choire, bearing to left for the first 100 feet.	An Garbh-choire.	2

Sgurr a' Choire Bhig, 2872, pron. *Sgurr a Corrie Vick* = peak of the little corrie, lies over $\frac{1}{2}$ m. E.S.E. of Sgurr nan Eag.

(a) From the summit a branch ridge runs off N.E., dividing An Garbh-choire from Coire Beag.

13	Coire nan Laogh	Dip, 2710. Descent into Coire nan Laogh, at first keep well up on slopes of Garsbheinn. Descent into Coire Beag difficult at first, keeping close under Sgurr a' Choire Bhig; then bearing well to right to avoid slabs.	Coire Beag (the small corrie).	2

Gars-Bheinn, 2934 (T.S.), pron. *Garsven* = the echoing mountain, lies 1 m. S.E. of Sgurr nan Eag.

(a) From a point a little S. of the summit a branch ridge runs off N.E., dividing Coire Beag from Coir a' Chruidh (corrie of the cattle), and terminating in a pinnacled crag at about 2125.

The main ridge from Gars-bheinn continues in the S.E. direction to Prominent point on ridge, 2665 ap. A little beyond this another branch ridge runs off N.E. into Coir' a' Chruidh, terminating at about 1850. Ridge continues E.S.E., with a prominent point at 2485 and another at the termination 2275.

5

Duirinish and Vaternish

(1)	**Healaval Mhor**	1538 ft.
(2)	**Healaval Bheag**	1601 ft.
(3)	**McLeod's Maidens**	207 ft.
(4)	**Waterstein Head**	967 ft.

Duirinish looks like the two elements of a lobster's claw about to close round the waters of Loch Dunvegan. Dunvegan is the starting and focal point, well supplied with hostelries, arts and crafts, camping ground, castle and historic relics. The Castle, built on the site of a Norse fortress of the ninth century is not architecturally magnificent, but has strong historical associations and is one of the oldest inhabited buildings in Scotland. For several hundred years it has been the home of the McLeods. The McLeods chose the McCrimmon family as their hereditary pipers, it was here around the end of the 16th century that the sophisticated form of bagpipe music known as piobaireachd (pibroch) was evolved. The gardens of the castle are douce and a pleasure to walk in. Of the various antiquities on view the most famous is the 'Fairy Flag', said to have been gifted to the Fourth Chief by the fairies. Waved in battle it summons supernatural aid for Clan McLeod, and may have its uses yet. Photos, 44, 46.

South Duirinish

The southern limb of the Duirinish claw is largely uninhabited territory. A short road runs south from Dunvegan to Orbost House, on Loch Bracadale, and continues unmetalled to lovely Varkasaig bay. The only other road eschews the mountainous centre, sending one branch up the east shore of Loch Dunvegan to Boreraig, where was the famous McCrimmon school of piping, and another westwards to Glendale and Neist Point. From Glendale a car track works south to Ramasaig. The whole S.W. shore is a line of magnificent cliffs, of which the greatest and most imposing is Waterstein Head.

Healaval Bheag (1601 ft. Lesser McLeod's Table)

Though the Bheag implies the lesser of the two peaks it is in fact the higher. To the viewer, as to the Gael, it simply appeared as a smaller table. The name is not simply due to its tabular summit. A local McLeod chief, Alaisdair Crotach, on one of his visits to the royal palace in Edinburgh rather discomfited a lowland earl by his gracious air and ease of manner. 'McLeod' said he, 'I'll wager nowhere in Skye have you seen a room so big and spacious, nor a roof so high, nor a table so rich, nor a candelabra so brilliant as in this palace of Holyrood.'

Alasdair Crotach invited him to Skye and spread a banquet on the flat summit of Healaveal Bheag. The sun was setting in blazing scarlet behind the Hebrides. Fifty clansmen stood around in a circle bearing flaming torches. Fifty square yards of the summit were spread with meats and wines. When the banquet finished in the early hours of the morning, Alasdair pointed to the star-lit sky and said, 'I ask you to agree with me, Sir, that my room is loftier than Holyrood's, this table greater than any to be found in the cities, and my clansmen more splendid than candelabra.' He made his point.

The ascent is best made from Varkasaig. The peak lies due west and is visible. Glen Varkasaig is now a forestry plantation, and a good track runs up the east side of the river. Once out of the trees two miles from Varkasaig at about the 500 ft. contour, one should strike directly for the summit (W.N.W.)

Healaval Mhor (1538 ft. Greater McLeod's Table)

Though the bulkier of the pair, this peak is the lower. It offers not quite so fine a viewpoint as Healaval Bheag. It is perhaps a little more accessible. It is most easily ascended up its E.N.E. ridge from Osdale croft which lies two miles south of Dunvegan off the Glendale road.

McLeod's Maidens

This name refers to three basaltic stacks lying off Idrigall Point at the mouth of Loch Bracadale. The highest is 207 ft. They are inaccessible by the shore, and landing by boat has its problems for here there is usually a heavy swell, and a considerable current. Roping down from the mainland cliffs affords the securest access. The rope (250 ft.) should be left in position. The middle stack was climbed many years ago by F. A. Evans. In 1959 I. S. Clough and J. McLean ascended the highest, mis-naming it the 'Old Lady'. At low tide there is no water between the shore and stack. The climb is severe. Climb to a ledge on the left, and trend right to a grassy patch with peg belay (50 ft.). Climb left along a gangway to a groove and so to a terrace at the foot of a wall (75 ft.). Climb the wall passing a big flake, to a ledge. Traverse left, and up a crack to the shoulder (75 ft.). Ascend ridge to summit block. See photo 41.

Waterstein

The great cliffs here give promise of many routes. Hardly any climbs have been recorded. Waterstein head is clearly the most impressive, though no record is known of its ascent from the seaward side. *The Green Lady*, a spire a mile north of Neist Point Lighthouse, high on the cliffs has been ascended. The climb starts at the S.E. corner and is severe. A road goes south to Ramasaig, giving convenient access to the sea cliffs to the south. Photo 43.

Vaternish and North Duirinish

This is a charming crofting area, full of variety but of little interest to the climber. Loch Bay separates Vaternish peninsula from North Duirinish. At An Dornell, the sound between the mainland and the Lampay isles, 4 miles N.N.E. of Dunvegan is a superb strand. Almost due north again on the west coast of Vaternish by Ardmore bay is Trumpan and the ruins of Trumpan church. In 1577 when the McLeod clan massacred many of the inhabitants of Eigg in a cave on that island, Clanranald plotted revenge. On a Sunday morning the next year, under cover of thick fog, when the people were at church, the invader surrounded the building, barred it, and set fire to it. Only one woman survived. The episode is recorded in a pibroch, Glengarry's March, in which there is one recurring discordant note – to simulate the screams of the victims.

6

Trotternish

(1)	**Sgurr Mor**	1600 ft. approx.
(2)	**Quirang**	1779 ft.
(3)	**Beinn Edra**	2003 ft.
(4)	**Sgurr a Madaidh Ruadha**	1926 ft.
(5)	**Baca Ruadh**	2091 ft.
(6)	**The Storr**	2358 ft.
(7)	**Beinn a Chearchuill**	1812 ft.
(8)	**Tianavaig**	1352 ft.

Trotternish comprises the two sonorous parishes of Kilmuir and Snizort, the index finger of Skye that points directly to the north. If the terrain and the seascapes fail to convey quite the same sense of Tir nan Og that the western peninsulas do, the spine of the peninsula certainly conveys its own bizarre quality. It is peppered with absurd pinnacles, most of which remain unclimbed, and its crest is close-cropped firm green-sward. These lie on a rib of hills that run from Sgurr Mor (1460 ft.) in the north to Beinn a' Chearchaill (1812 ft.), some 19 miles, considerably longer than the Cuillin main ridge and involving 7700 feet of ascent. The east side is one long escarpment, only at certain points scalable by the walker. The one-inch O.S. maps marks 'bealachs' where there are practicable walking routes from the east side to a col.

A road circumnavigates the peninsula. Starting from Portree it runs along the east coast, never far from the sea though often far above it. At Lealt, a decomposing metalled road branches inland to 600 ft. at Loch Cuithir, convenient to some of the southern hills (no signpost). Just before Elishader the road comes close to the sea, and from near here one may see the so-called 'kilt rock' named because the stripes on the basaltic cliffs are thought to depict the pleats of a kilt. At Brogaig is Staffin bay, a good road ['Bealach Road'] takes to the hill, and eventually crosses the spine of the peninsula at 850 ft. and drops down by the river Rha to Uig in the west. Beyond Brogaig and to the left is the Quirang, whose many needles remain inviolate. The region west of the road is extraordinarily tumultuous. Small hills hide behind escarpments and lochans lurk beneath the hills. The road continues north to Kilmaluag, and hits the west coast by old Duntulm castle, the ancient seat of McDonald of the Isles. The west side of the peninsula is less interesting, and the ascent of the hilly spine is less attractive from this side. From Uig the road runs to the head of Loch Snizort, and either east to Portree or west to Dunvegan. The central spine is always accessible without technical difficulty on the west side. Trotternish is the driest end of the Island.

Sgurr Mor (1460 ft. Big Peak)

South of Kilmaluag an escarpment of hills is seen to rise suddenly out of the low moor. The most northerly and prominent of these is Sgurr Mor. It is most readily ascended from Donnista croft (200 ft.) half a mile south of Kilmalnag. The distance to Sgurr Mor is 2 miles.

Quirang (1779 ft.)

The name is said to be derived from the Gaelic Cuith-raing, meaning pillared stronghold. Close under the crest of Meall nan Suireamach (the true summit) the upper cliffs have slipped down to form a corrie in which pinnacles lean out at crazy angles (see photos 49 and 50). Around the base of the corrie low conical hills hide the intervening valley, the true Quirang, from the shore road, but it is well seen from the hill road to Uig. There are several lochs hereabouts, of which Loch Langaig, by the road near Floddigarry, is the finest in Skye, and forms a superb foreground to the view south of the Quirang.

The shortest access to the base of the cliffs is to take the hill [Bealach] road to Uig (turn off main road at Brogaig) up to about the 600 ft. contour. The Quirang valley reveals itself on the north and the way up is obvious.

Meall nan Suireamach is climbed in 30 minutes from the 850 ft. col on this road.

The most attractive approach is to go by Loch Langaig which lies 300 yards S.W. of the shore road, but is not visible from it. A good track runs north and west of the loch towards the Quirang. One can see breaches in the escarpment to the west.

Bealach Road to Bealach Uige

From the Bealach road from Brogaig to Uig at the col (850 ft.). Meall nan Suireamach is easily accessible, thus leading to the top of the Quirang cliffs. Southwards a gentle rise takes one onto Biod Buidhe (1523 ft.). Beyond that the escarpment becomes undistinguished, and moorland of no great interest rises to the mound of Druim na Coille (1058 ft.) via the two passes of Bealach na Coiseachan to the north and the Bealach Uige to the south. This part of the ridge is not easily gained from the east, for several miles of boggy moorland separate it from Staffin, or even the rough road up Kilmartin river. It is, however, relatively accessible from Uig by a road that runs east up Glen Uig on the north side to the 700 ft. contour. It leaves the main road just south of the Post Office. From here to Kilmaluag or Floddigarry makes a pleasant traverse of eleven miles.

Beinn Edra (2003 ft.)

This peak shows a moorland slope to Uig, and a broken escarpment falling from the summit on the east side. The peak is accessible from the road up the northside of Glen Uig by the track that runs towards Bealach Uige. The approach from the east is relatively arduous, the nearest access being where the croft road crosses the Kilmartin river just before Marishadder. The three miles across the moor will take a good deal longer than three miles usually do.

South of Beinn Edra the escarpment continues over a series of small peaks and bealachs, gentle on the west, steep but broken on the east to another high point, Craig a' Lain (1995 ft.). This point on the ridge is relatively easily gained, for a metalled road (poor repair) runs west from Lealt on the Portree–Staffin road up to Loch Cuithir, at which point the peak is only one mile distant, and 1300 ft. above.

Sgurr a' Mhadaidh Ruadh (1926 ft. Peak of the Red Fox)

Immediately west stands the prow of Sgurr a' Mhadaidh Ruadh (1926 ft. Peak of the Red Fox), which presents a Matterhorn shape from Lealt glen. It may be climbed by its S.S.E. ridge with slight complications at two short bands of rock. The north ridge is steep and buttressed for 800 ft., but no routes are recorded. Pleasant grass slopes lead from Loch Cuithir to either summit. There is a great deal of unclimbed rock hereabouts [see photo 51].

Baca Ruadh (2091 ft.)

This peak is also best ascended from the east using the Lealt road, leaving it where the river turns south. An eastward spur affords a stimulating airy route to the top. The north and south faces are steep and craggy. It presents no problem from the west. The road up the north bank of Hinnisdal (a mile south Uig) leads one by a pleasant winding river to Coire Fuar and its gentle upper slopes. It is four miles to the summit.

Bealach Hartaval

This col between the Storr and Baca Ruadh to the north affords a magnificent prospect north and south. The flanks are close cropped greensward. Coming from the north one should keep along the ridge (Sgurr a' Mhadaidh) till slightly south of the col, and then descend. In this way the crags are avoided.

The Storr (2358 ft.)

South of Baca Ruadh the escarpment trends east as well as south, so that by the time the Storr is reached the Portree–Staffin road is only one mile distant. This escarpment is made prominent by the leaning pinnacle to its east, the Old Man of Storr. It is particularly well seen when travelling north on the road from Sligachan to Portree. The cliffs of the Storr are high, over 500 ft., and are split by black gullies into five buttresses, all of which are vertical or over-hanging. Storr in gaelic is said to mean a 'high cliff' or 'decayed tooth'. Both descriptions are apt, and no one has yet successfully tackled the rotten buttresses. Below the cliffs stand not only the Old Man, but a dozen tottering fantastically shaped pinnacles. It is an old scene, for the stones bear the symbolism of some ancient pictish circle, conveying their own morbid atmosphere. Yet they spring from a corrie lined with a brilliant greensward sparkling with flowers and bird-song. There is none of the sinister impact that Callinish in Lewis conveys. Only two routes have been recorded in this corrie, both on the Old Man itself. It is a 160 ft. of weather and pock-marked light grey basalt offering very little security to the climber. The base overhangs on all sides. Photo 52.

The original route was led in 1955 by Don Whillans with J. Barber and G. J. Sutton, making a 220 ft. V.S. Start at the north side, and climb 20 ft. to a circular hole in the rock. Traverse left

49.
Quirang
Pinnacles.

50. Quirang Pinnacles.

51. Sgurr à Mhadaidh Ruadh from the Lealt to Loch Cuithir road.

52. The Storr pinnacles and Loch Leathan from the north

(crux) to gain prominent nose in centre of face. It is strenuous, loose and very severe. Climb to a grassy cave directly above, and then to shattered blocks on the east side of the pinnacle. The rest is easy. Descend by two rappels, and 200 feet of rope is needed.

The Portree face was climbed in 1967 by G. B. Lee, and P. Thomson (220 ft. V.S.). This face has a 20 ft. pillar at its foot, which is used to gain the overhanging wall above it to gain a cave. Traverse right into a steep groove and climb to a peg below an overhang. Step left to foot of steep crack and climb this for a few feet. Make a hard move right, and go up an obvious traverse line left and around the arete to a peg belay in the final crack, which is ascended to gain the summit. Descent of the lower section has to be by rappel.

The direct approach is by an excellent beaten track, occasionally boggy lower down, that leaves the Portree–Staffin road at the north end of Loch Leathan where overhead electricity lines cross the road.

The main peak can be gained from the corrie either by traversing south under the cliffs to Coire Faoin, followed by the ascent of grass and scree to the plateau south of the summit. A more scenic route is to traverse along this cliff-base to a gap to the north (north col). From here the view back to the pinnacles, Tianavaig, the Sound of Raasay and the distant Cuillin is superb and dramatic. To gain the summit cross through the gap, and trend left and up till easy ground enables one to regain the top of the escarpment of cliffs above the north col. As one ascends the view south becomes steadily more spectacular. The summit is attained by broaching the upper line of crags at one of many gullies.

The north col can be attractively reached by walking up the Rigg burn which crosses the road 2½ miles north of Loch Leathan. It leads to a lovely greensward corrie.

The summit may also be reached from the south by climbing to Lochan a' Bhealach Bhig, above which there is a break in the escarpment. Bealach Bhig is marked on the O.S. map.

The Storr may be conveniently taken in in the course of a hill walk starting at Borve or Lealt.

Beinn a' Chearchaill (1812 ft.)

This peak is the south end of the ridge, and lies very close to the road at Loch Fhada (450 ft.), from which it may be easily ascended. A gentle walk leads north to the Storr. It may also be gained by a longer but more attractive route from Borve on the Portree–Uig road choosing the line up the ridge marked 'Pein Borve'. One may take a car to the 400 ft. contour by taking a north running road just east of Borve.

Beinn Tianavaig (1352 ft.)

The ascent of this superb viewpoint has more to recommend it than would at first sight appear. Seen from the Portree–Sligachan road it looks like just another dull boggy hill. Only on close inspection does one find that its southerly and easterly slopes are composed of porous gravel upon which grows a firm dry turf and the greatest selection of wild flowers one can hope to find on any one hillside in Skye. The summit falls away abruptly in an east facing escarpment, below which dry grassy hollows and slopes run down to the shore.

The mountain is best climbed by taking the B893 to Braes two miles south of Portree. After crossing a bleak moor with Tianavaig directly ahead of one, the road drops down to the west shore of Raasay Sound, and some of the lushest and most sheltered terrain in Skye. Take the turning marked 'Camastianavaig' (actually Camus Tianavaig, Tianavaig Creek) and take to the hill at the burn that runs down by the most northerly of the croft houses. By following this line, the ground is dry underfoot the whole way to the summit (40 minutes), even after heavy rain. In summer, unfortunately, there is a good deal of bracken, which is on the increase.

The summit has a survey point. It offers a spectacular view of Portree, making it well worth a nocturnal visit, and is in one of the island's finest vantage points. There are rocks, but loose and useless for climbing.

The road down to Loch Sligachan at Peinchorran is well worth travelling, and a good path links the road-end with Sligachan.

This region is called the Braes, and was the scene of a famous fight put up by crofters, who while resisting eviction, rolled stones down the brae above the road onto the forces of order.

Neighbouring Islands

Ascrib Islands

This archipelago of islands lies in the mouth of Loch Snozrt, in the Parish of Duirinish, one and a half miles east of Vaterstein peninsula. The number of reefs is largely determined by the state of the tide, but stand well above high tide, in particular the five named islands: South Ascrib (134 ft.), Eilean Geary, Sgeir à Chapuil, Eileen Creagach, and Eilean Losal. The group is composed of tertiary basalt, capped with a friable soil, a haven for burrowing puffins. A boat may be hired from Uig. Enquire either at Uig hotel or the Post Office.

There is no habitation on the island.

Soay

Soay, the hour-glass shaped island, beckons no one. Directly S.W. of Gars-Bheinn, it catches the drips off the Cuillins. Seen from the sea it is low and unspectacular. Seen from the mountains above it seems to be so riddled with lochans that it ought by rights to sink. In fact it is a jewel. In the slender waist of the hour glass are two bays, each perfect harbours a mere three hundred yards apart, yet respectively facing Skye and facing the mainland. In this sheltered defile grow a profusion of bushes and trees, and lurk quiet little cottages, some inhabited, but most untenanted. The island was once the scene of a thriving shark fishery. A boat calls every second Tuesday (phone Mallaig 33, Bruce Watt). It has a radio telephone.

Scalpay

Scalpay (Skye) is not to be confused with the more famous Scalpay (Harris). The name means 'Cave Island'. Situated 3 miles N.W. of Broadford, less than two hundred yards of water separate it at low tide. Here at Caolas (pron: Kyles) Scalpay there is a navigation light, and to its east a pier with a road leading round to Scalpay house.

The island is inaccessible by public transport. It is of most interest to those who collect islands, or who seek an eyrie off the coast of Skye. The highest point, 1298 ft. Mullach nan Carn is the island's most accessible point and only eminence. The rocks, mainly Torridonian, with intrusions of granite, form only a few small crags.

Pabbay

Pabbay, the Hermit Island, is a common enough Hebridean name. The Skye Pabbay lies one mile off the mainland of Skye, two miles from Broadford. It is flat and featureless, rising only to 89 ft. It is run as a farm. There are some holiday cottages to let on the island. Its very flatness and its location impart to it a certain attractive tranquillity.

Raasay

Raasay is an island of great character, varied in topography and with much to interest the visitor. Here was born John McKay and his son Angus, two of the finest pipers and composers of all time. Its west side, facing Skye, is the most sheltered and most populated. The island is 13 miles long. At its nearest point, Skye lies half a mile across the Narrows of Raasay, where there is a remarkable boot-shaped peninsula. There is no harbour on the Skye side, but on Raasay Churchton Bay provides shelter for small boats. Many houses ring the bay, and there are fine stands of trees. The road runs south along the coast past Inverarish to Suisnish point, where there is a pier at which mail steamers call. There used to be an old iron ore mine. It ceased working in 1919. A rough road continues round the south end of the island to Eyre, at Eyre Point, and then degenerates into a track that links at South Fearns with a road track coming over the moor from Inverarish.

The remainder of the east coast up to Brochel is uninhabited. It is fine country with a long escarpment, Druim an Aonaich, running at about the 800 ft. contour. Below the cliffs steep grass slopes run into the sea. A path runs along the shore. South of Brochel is a fine steep buttress. Above this escarpment, and three miles from Inverarish stands Dun Caan (1456 ft.), the island's highest point. Two paths, one from South Fearns, and one from Inverarish lead to the summit. These paths are useful, because the heavy faulting in the island has produced areas of subsidence, and therefore of bog, which are hard to cross, and a direct crossing of the moor would be extremely tedious.

Dun Caan has a fine but truncated top, whose characteristic appearance is recognisable from many points in Skye and the mainland. It has the irritating habit of being in sunshine when Cuillin peaks are drenched in rain, and is well worth an off-day visit for the climber. The view is superb, the more so because the immediate environment is so delightful. Boswell is said to have danced a jig on the flat summit.

At Inverarish is Raasay House (now an hotel), and close by is the entrance to an old semi-artificial cave, Uamh nan Ramph. Higher up is a hill, often referred to as Temptation Hill, for it was the view from here that tempted one man to become proprietor. Also close to the house is the ancient St. Maol-Luag's chapel. Pictish stones have also been found hereabouts.

Around the House and Inverarish there are fine oak woodlands, and the atmosphere of the whole place is one of lushness contrasting with the bare Skye moorlands. A good road goes northwards, leaving the shore and passing over the moorland at the high point of 769 ft. to drop down on the east side at Brochel where Torridonian conglomerate pokes through the Lewisian gneiss. Here is another fine stand of woodland. The northern tip of the island is a tortured terrain with, on the west side, some wonderful bays and coves. A path leads over to Ardnish and Torrin, but scarcely anyone lives there now. It continues to the northerly point opposite South Rona.

Raasay still enjoys a four times weekly service in both directions by the mail steamer plying between Kyle of Lochalsh and Portree, from either of which it is equally accessible. By taking the morning steamer from Portree and the afternoon steamer back one can get seven hours on the island. A private boat may be hired from Sconser or Peinchorran. (Tel. Raasay 226). A car may be hired. (Tel. Raasay 206).

South Rona

South Rona is close to Raasay, separated by Coalas Rona, whose half mile is broken up with two islands. This remote island is geologically a continuation of North Raasay – Lewisian gneiss with felspar dykes. It is a rough little island, all crag and bog. The remains of the old Kirk, An Teampull, can be descried at the south extremity. A good path runs the length of the island up to the lighthouse at the north end, where at Loch na Braige is a pier.

The island's main peak is Meall Ascarseid (406 ft.). To its N.E. on the east coast is Ascarseid Tioram, or Dry Harbour, once the main centre of population. The people abandoned the island after the end of the First World War, and forcibly took possession of crofts in Raasay, though for another 20 years one family continued to raise cattle operating from Ascarseid Mhor, the harbour on the west side. Ascarseid Mhor is a delightful little fjord, and superb harbour for small boats. Pink felspar cliffs drop steeply into the water, and small lush woodland lends a touch of luxury.

Trodday

Trodday lies one mile north of Skye, and 3 miles N.W. lies Fladdachuain. Both isles are uninhabited. They are noteworthy for their hexagonal basalt columns, similar to Trotternish.

Graded List of Rock Climbs

These climbs are indicated in the text as being of some interest.

MODERATE

N.E. ridge, Garsbheinn 88
N.E. ridge, Sgurr a Choire Bhig 88
East ridge, Sgurr Dubh Beag (without traverse) 90
Inaccessible Pinnacle, East ridge 97
Pinnacle ridge, Sgurr nan Gillean 111
Foxes Rake 119
Banachdich Gully 122
N. Buttress, Sgumain 130
Zig-zag 133
Collie's route, Cioch 134
Amphitheatre Arête 135
West Gully, Coire an Laoigh 140

DIFFICULT

Sgurr a Choire Bhig gullies 88
Sgurr Dubh Beag traverse 90
South Twin 100
Terrace Buttress 101
Collie's S.E. Climb 101
S.E. Buttress, Sgurr a Mhadaidh 104
Harta face, An Caisteal 104
Am Bhasteir, Lota Corrie 108
Naismith's Climb 108
Am Bhasteir Chimney 122
N.W. Buttress, Sgurr a Mhadaidh 119
Hamish's Chimney 120
Vanishing Gully 121
Branching Gully 121
Window Buttress 123

VERY SEVERE

INDEX

INDEX

INDEX